THE FIRE Inside

James L. Giles

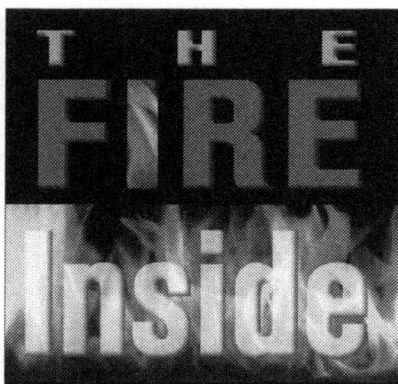

James L. Giles

Unless otherwise noted, Scripture quotations are from the King James Version of the Bible. Scripture quotations marked NIV are taken from the New International Version of the Bible. Copyright © 1973, 1978, 1984 International Bible Society. Used by permission of Zondervan Bible Publishers.

Copyright © 2004 James L. Giles
ISBN 1-56229-167-X

Pneuma Life Publishing, Inc.
12138 Central Ave Ste 251
Mitchellville, Maryland 20721
301-390-3680
http://www.pneumalife.com

Printed in the United States of America

CONTENTS

"Every person is a creative genius at something. Every artist is less a kind of person than every person is a special kind of artist. Being creative is what makes us 'in God's image.' We are all creatologists. Every one of us must be an innovator, an inventor, a creative genius. These creatology titles are no longer reserved for a select few, but for every single one of us—whether we like it or not."

—Leonard Sweet

"An education is not the filling of a pail, it is the lighting of a fire."

—William Butler Yeats

DEDICATION

This Book is dedicated to all those committed to creating the future.

INTRODUCTION

Some refer to it as a calling, purpose or destiny. However you put it, God puts every person on the earth to achieve something noteworthy. However, don't confuse achievement with celebrity or fame. A celebrity is someone who is famous for being famous. Instead I am talking about something much deeper, the fire inside, in the deepest part of you. It burns with unquenchable intensity. Every cell in your being is consumed with the passion for something. It may be music, physics, poetry, painting, architecture, teaching, writing, parenting, cooking, writing software, starting a company, running for congress, building a great church, becoming the top salesperson in the company you work for or any one of a thousand other things.

This is not simply a wish or fantasy. You have a raging fire inside that will not leave you alone. You must respond or pay a dear price. That's because God has created you to succeed. He has endowed you with amazing capacities and made available to you the miraculous force of faith. God put His will in your heart and gave you the drive and patience to accomplish what was predestined for you.

In this book, you will learn about these amazing capabilities that God has given you so that you can achieve your destiny. You will learn about the power of your magnificent brain, your marvelous mind, your powerful memory. You will learn about your intelligence and giftedness. Furthermore, you will learn about the force of creativity, the steps to becoming a master learner and the phenomenon of genius. After reading this book, you will learn that God has fully equipped you to stoke that fire inside of you. You will be well on your way to fulfilling your purpose.

1

YOUR AMAZING BRAIN

Welcome Aboard! I have the privilege of being your captain on a fascinating journey through the latest research on the amazing brain—one of the awesome tools God has given us to accomplish what is predestined for our lives. Your brain contains approximately forty-eight ounces of tissue containing one trillion (that's a one with twelve zeros) brain cells, neurons, axons and dendrites. The neuron, the basic unit of the brain, is a complex information processing system. Each of your approximately one hundred billion neurons can process up to fifty thousand messages per second. Researchers say that every second of our lives our amazing brains are processing several billion bits of information. Think about that. Your brain generates enough power to light a small light bulb—about twenty watts—while you are awake.

As you are reading this book, up to one million impulses are rushing through your brain at up to two hundred fifty miles per hour. At some point, the numbers become almost absurd and serve as an analog to your understanding of just how complex and powerful your amazing brain is. Russian neurologist Pyotr Anokhin has attempted to calculate the number of possible connections in the normal human brain. What he came up with: a 1 followed by 6,213,710 miles of zeros, and he thinks this figure may be too low. Neurologist Richard Restak believes that the number of possible connections in the brain's neuronal system is more than the total number of atoms in the universe. It is said that the complexity of the world's entire telephone system is equivalent to a part of your brain the size of a pea.

How are those millions of messages processed in the brain? First the neuron receives the message and processes it inside the cell body. Then, by way of long fibers extending from the cell body of the neuron through the shorter fibers called dendrites, the message is sent to other neurons. The messages are transmitted chemically across small gaps called synapses. A synapse is like a bridge between neurons. It is a very smart bridge because the synapse determines whether a message gets transmitted. Synapses are also important because they are where learning and memory occur.

In the course of one day, adults lose about one hundred thousand brain cells due to the aging process. However, research shows that if you were to lose ten thousand brain cells per minute for eighty years, you only would have lost about three percent of your brain's neuronal capacity. With its multiple biochemical and biophysical interactions, along with its ability to handle enormous quantities of information, your brain is far more complex than any computer.

In the next twenty-four hours, with absolutely no effort on your part, your brain and subconscious mind will:

• Cause you to breathe twenty-three thousand times, inhaling and exhaling 438 cubit feet of air.

• Cause your heart to beat one hundred thousand times, a rate that would add up to about 2.5 billion times in seventy years.

• Cause your heart to pump 4,300 gallons of blood, enough to fill thirteen million barrels over the course of a lifetime. Cause your blood to make 1,450 complete circuits through six hundred thousand miles of capillaries.

The brain is truly an amazing creation of God. You and I are made in the image of God. King David wrote in Psalm 139:14: "Thank you for making me so wonderfully complex! Your workmanship is marvelous" (NLT).

As simple and inelegant as it seems to Darwinists, man was created by God in His own image. It is the breath of God that is to be the animating principle of the brain and mind of man. After God formed man from the dust of the ground, his form was without life. All his organs, including the brain, and systems were in place. However, it was not until God breathed into his nostrils the breath of life that man became a sentient, feeling, thinking, conscious, perceiving being. The optimal function of the brain and mind are part of the divine design of God, as such they are certainly included in His redemptive plan.

Your one brain is comprised of the brain stem, limbic system and neocortex. There are two hemispheres, left and right, separated by a thick fibrous band called the corpus callosum. Here is a general description of the functions of the brain's parts:

The Brain Stem

Located at the base of the skull, the brain stem controls basic functions such as breathing, heart rate, and the fight/flight response when danger threatens. The brain stem is an extension of the spinal cord. There is a swelling on it called the medulla oblongata. The medulla oblongata is what controls our life-support systems.

The Limbic System

Limbic is from the Latin word meaning collar. The limbic system wraps around the brain stem like a collar. Its key components are the hypothalamus and the amygdala. The limbic system is your emotional control center. It helps to maintain a stable environment within the body. The hypothalamus and the amygdala also regulate goal-setting behaviors and regulate the emotions. Health and memory also are believed to be controlled by the limbic system.

This is interesting because the Bible teaches that there is a relationship between the emotions and health. "A merry heart doeth good like a medicine: but a broken spirit drieth the bones" (Proverbs 17:22, KJV).

Modern research into brain-based learning leads us to see the limbic system is involved. The brain does not split learning into cognitive and affective modes. The emotions play a significant role in the phenomenon of learning. When the brain is in a state of positive emotional arousal, it releases opiate-like chemicals called endorphins. The release of the endorphins triggers the release of powerful neurotransmitters called acetycholines. Remember, it is in the synapses where learning and memory take place. This is important because the acetycholines lubricate the spaces between the neurons, the synapses. The limbic system also contains the thalamus, which monitors and sorts messages from the senses so we do not become confused. The pituitary gland controls the release of hormones allowing our bodies to produce energy from the foods we eat. The pineal gland, which is responsible for the rate at which our bodies grow and mature, and the hippocampus, which forms and stores new memories, all are contained within the limbic system.

Also at the upper part of the brain stem is what is called the Reticular Activating System, or RAS. It is a master alarm bell that alerts the brain to incoming information from the senses. Without the RAS, we would all be comatose. The RAS is only about the size of your little finger. It functions as a filter, allowing certain messages access to the neocortex faster than others. Your RAS would react more quickly to information that your child had fallen from her bicycle than it would to the news of who had won the World Series. In some inexplicable way, the RAS knows what is important. It is the RAS that filters out sensory stimuli so you can concentrate on final exams, or on solving some complex math or physics problem. Superior athletes develop control over their RAS so as not to become distracted by what is going on around them during a competition.

The Neocortex

This is the so-called intelligent brain. All of the higher intelligences—seeing, hearing, thinking, talking and creating—are handled in the neocortex. We organize the world, store experiences in memory, produce and understand speech, hear and appreciate music, and see and appreciate art via the neocortex. The brain of a six-month-old baby is already one-half its adult weight. The brain of a two and a half-year-old child is three-fourths its adult weight, and the brain of a five-year-old child is nine-tenths its adult weight. It was discovered in the 1950s that newborns see quite well and begin to perceive forms and patterns during the first hours of life. From the moment of birth, an infant is fascinated by the things in his or her world and begins to explore them immediately. The neocortex takes up about eighty-five percent of the brain's total mass and is divided into two halves, or hemispheres. Each hemisphere contains networks of cells that receive, store and retrieve information. When the terms "left brain" and "right brain" are used, they are referring to the two hemispheres of the neocortex. It is here where we reason and solve problems.

Left Hemisphere of the Neocortex

Commonly referred to as the left brain, this hemisphere specializes in the so-called academic aspects of learning—language, mathematics, logic, sequence and analysis, speech, writing.

Right Hemisphere of the Neocortex

The right brain, as it is called, specializes in the so-called creative processes—music, rhyme and rhythm, visual impressions, color, pictures and images, metaphors, analogies and patterns. Conceptuality is also ascribed to the right hemisphere. It is in this hemisphere that ideas such as truth, beauty and loyalty are processed.

Each hemisphere is dominant in certain activities. However, recent research says that we learn most effectively when both hemispheres of the neocortex are involved. Some people are left-brain, or "linear," learners. These people prefer the methodical, step-by-step build-up of information. Others are right-brain, or "global," learners. They want the big picture.

The research of professor Robert Ornstein revealed a complementary relationship between the hemispheres of the neocortex. Dr. Ornstein found that when the "weaker" side of the brain was stimulated and encouraged to work with the "stronger" side, there was a net increase in overall performance. You would think the increase would be double—$1+1=2$, 1 representing the left hemisphere, and 1 representing the right hemisphere of the neocortex. However, the overall increase in performance was closer to $1+1=5$.

Despite these dramatic results, schools across America and the Western world emphasize left-brain learning. We learn the three R's—reading, writing and arithmetic—all left-hemisphere functions. Textbooks are almost all written in black and white, yet we know that the brain processes images in color and that learning is enhanced when visuals, color and music are used. We also know now that intelligence is not static or psychometric. In fact, Howard Gardner of Harvard University has shown that there are multiple intelligences, which we all possess to some degree. (See more on intelligence in Chapter 3.)

We know that intelligence is not solely a factor of genetics. An enriched learning environment stimulates changes in the chemical makeup of the neurons. A rich learning environment affects other brain cells called glial cells. Glial cells glue your brain together. They, unlike neurons, can split apart and duplicate themselves. When glial cells split, axons push through and form connections to other neurons. The richer your environment, the faster these glial cells split. A rich learning environment may have been the reason well-known geniuses such as Albert Einstein became geniuses.

When California research scientist Dr. Marian Diamond found the brain of professor Albert Einstein in a freezer in Kansas, she found something startling. Dr. Diamond and her associates examined the part of Einstein's brain responsible for math thinking and found many more glial cells than most of us have in that part of our brain.

Einstein did not consider himself a mathematician. He was a theoretical physicist who despised the experimental method and believed that imagination was more important than knowledge. Einstein's imaginary trip through the universe on a light beam was a function of the right hemisphere. He then used the left side of his brain for the physics and mathematics to explain what his imagination had perceived. Einstein also participated in split-hemispheric activities such as playing the violin and the piano.

Later in Einstein's career, he became more sophisticated in mathematics. David Hilbert, a mathematician, contemporary and admirer of Einstein who came close to some of Einstein's early insights into general relativity, assessed Einstein's mathematical ability. Hilbert said: "Every boy in the streets of Gottingen understands more about four-dimensional geometry than Einstein. Yet, in spite of that, Einstein did the work, and not the mathematicians." Abraham Pais, an Einstein biographer, notes that the intuitive and visual methods used so copiously and with such great results suffered as he became more proficient in and reliant upon mathematics.

Like Einstein, another great scientist, Michael Faraday, had the intuition and imagination of a genius. Faraday, universally acknowledged as one of the greatest physicists of all time, was not a mathematician. Faraday (1791-1867), a Christian, was a self-taught genius from a poor family. Isaac Asimov in his History of Physics wrote, "Faraday..., perhaps the greatest electrical innovator of all, was completely innocent of mathematics..." It was Faraday who originated the concepts of electromagnetic lines of force and the invisible electromagnetic field. Faraday, a deeply spiritual man and an active member of his family's Sandemanian church, preferred to call himself a philosopher. Even though he was responsible for a great number of discoveries in the fields of physics and chemistry, he did not choose to be called a scientist.

It was Faraday's visualization of the concepts of electromagnetic force and electromagnetic field that James Clerk Maxwell, another Christian, developed a comprehensive theoretical and mathematical framework to further explain. Maxwell was one of the principal mathematicians of his day.

This did not, however, prevent him from seeing the elegant genius in the work of Faraday. Maxwell said that in his initial studies of electricity, he read no mathematics until he had finished reading Faraday's *Experimental Researches in Electricity*.

Einstein, Faraday and Maxwell were all visual thinkers who used the power of the right hemisphere to imagine what might be.

Faraday greatly influenced Einstein. Maxwell died the year Einstein was born, 1879. As a child, he, like Einstein, had been considered a poor student. (See more on this topic in Chapter 3.) Between 1897 and 1900, when Einstein was a student at the Zurich Polytechnic, he found his physics professor, Heinrich Weber, boring and often cut class to read Faraday and Maxwell. On the wall of Einstein's Princeton study were pictures of Isaac Newton, Faraday and Maxwell.

Just as we have shown that great scientists have heavily drawn upon the right hemisphere's intuitive and imaginative powers; great artists such as Picasso and Cezanne drew upon the left hemisphere of their brains in a lot of their approach to art. Examination of the notebooks of artists such as Picasso, Cezanne and DaVinci reveal mathematical and geometric descriptions of what they were trying to accomplish as artists. The notebooks of DaVinci, who was also an inventor, reveal detailed drawings of various prototype machines.

Although these famous scientists and artists enjoyed incredible achievements, none of them were born with any more neurons than you were. However, they may have been privileged to inhabit an enriched environment. This is an environment full of stimulating learning opportunities.

It does not cost a lot of money to expose a child to this kind of enrichment. Children are naturally curious about the world. Nature is the greatest university for them—and it's free. Simply explaining how things work or finding out together how things work is stimulating for the child. As well, reading, listening to music (classical music has been shown to stimulate the brain waves involved in learning), drawing, painting and playing an instrument are all enriching activities.

It doesn't matter how old you are, the number of possible neuronal connections in your brain is greater than the number of stars in the universe. Neurobiologists say that it simply is not true that we lose up to 100,000 neurons each year. Professors from Stanford and the Albert Einstein College of Medicine, Yeshiva University have said that as we grow old, the brain does not necessarily lose cells. It is true, however, that as we grow old, brain cells may shrink or become dormant. But if we continue to stimulate our brains, they form new connections and dendrites continue to develop. The same thing that facilitates growth in the brain of an infant stimulates activity in the brain of an older person, and that's an enriched environment.

Therefore, you should never stop challenging your brain. Learn new things. Try things with increasing levels of difficulty. Your brain possesses a quality called elasticity. This means that the structure of the brain is altered through enriching experiences. No matter your age, sex, color or background, you have an incredible capacity to learn. Your brain is hard-wired by God to:

- Detect patterns and make approximations.

- Exert a phenomenal capacity for several types of memory.

- Self-correct and learn from experience by way of analysis of external data and self-reflection.

- Possess an almost inexhaustible capacity to create.

When your brain is repeatedly stimulated, the existing synaptic connections are strengthened among the brain cells and the creation of new connections is stimulated. Children should be exposed to an array of interesting stimuli. Children should be allowed to determine to a large degree what is interesting. Cognitive development already has begun in infants by the age of eight or nine months. You should enrich the environment. You should do the same for yourself. Recapture your fascination for things. What did you love as a child that you eventually lost interest in? Find and rekindle your passion. That in itself is not enough, though. You need commitment. Successful achievement, invention, innovation, discovery, creativity and mastery do not yield to the impatient. Whatever you do, make it fun. Fun is neuronal rocket fuel.

You need to come down with what I call chronic Episodic Idea Attack, or EIA. Challenge yourself to think in fresh ways, on new levels, about different things. Take out some pink, purple, blue or green paper and a colored pen. Turn the paper sideways or upside down and begin to generate solutions to problems. Go to a stimulus-rich environment, maybe to a park, and write. Then think and write more. Draw pictures of the solutions. Be as graphic as you can. Force yourself to think in new ways. Buy five magazines and five books you thought you weren't interested in. Listen to Mozart or Beethoven. Turn off the television. Listen to some clean comedy, for laughter stimulates positive brain activity. Refuse to be bored. Passion is a choice. So is commitment. There are a million things in this world that will fascinate you. Choose one and get on with it.

2

THE DANCING MIND

Your mind works in a harmonious relationship with your brain. Chungliang Al Huang has written that the dancing mind is "relaxed, visionary and open to the full range of human possibility." Jesus Christ Himself said all things are possible to him that believeth (Matthew 17:20, 19:26; Mark 9:23, 11:22-24). The human mind energized by faith is the most powerful force for good or evil among men. The mind is that part of us where we will, feel, think and reason.

One of the Greek words for mind, nous, means the place of will, disposition, resolve and decision. Disposition means one's total inner attitude. The mind is the place where we know that which is knowable through the senses. The mind is the seat of counsel and opinion. Nous denotes powers of spiritual perception and the capacity for intellectual apprehension. The mind, according to the Greeks, also means insight and inventiveness.

No one has ever seen a mind, but all around us are the evidences of the powers of the mind. Your mind works in a harmonious relationship with your brain and places at your disposal vast intellectual and creative resources. It is my belief that God gave man a mind with such enormous potential so that he might carry out His command that man exercise dominion over all the earth. In his book Biblical Creationism, scientist and Christian apologist Dr. Henry Morris wrote this:

In order to "subdue" the earth, as they were directed, the (created man) would have to learn about its systems and processes (thus developing what we now call "science"), then to organize and utilize this knowledge in productive ways that would both benefit others and honor their Creator ("technology"), and then to disseminate this information and its products to everyone ("business," "education," "communication," "transportation," etc.). God said five times that different aspects of His creation were "good" and then finally, after it was all complete, pronounced it all "very good" (Genesis 1:31). This divine evaluation could be received and then detailed by man in works of music, art and literature, glorifying and praising God for all He had done in creating and making all things.

(Morris, 1993, Baker Book House, p. 21)

According to Dr. Morris, the impulse to study the laws of nature ("science") was placed in man by God at the creation. Theoretical and experimental physics, astronomy, ornithology, aerodynamics, biology, archaeology, meteorology, ichthyology and medicine are all areas where our knowledge of how and why things work is expanded. There are yet things to say through various artistic media.

Modern research has demythologized genius and intelligence. It has placed into the hands of everyday people tools with which they may significantly strengthen their own capabilities and enhance their performance in specific areas. Not everyone will be an Albert Einstein. However, because of what we now know about the brain, multiple intelligence, the myth of global giftedness, genius and human potential, practically everyone may perform at levels once only reserved for those believed to be genetically or environmentally gifted.

You and I were born with a profound capacity and drive to learn. We were fascinated with everything in our environment. Along with the drive to learn, we came into the world with a joy for learning. Babies are little scientists and inventors. They are wired to investigate everything around them, and if left with materials, they will transform them into something of their own design. Experts say that from birth, children are faced with problem-solving tasks and seek information to help solve them. Psychologist Michael Schulman says children seek to solve these four basic problems:

1) What's out there?

2) What leads to what?

3) What makes things happen?

4) What's controllable?

It is the function of the child's intelligence to solve these problems repeatedly over the course of their childhood. As adults, the same four categories challenge our intelligence.

By eight or nine months old, sometimes earlier, cognitive development already has begun in a child. In fact, the brain and nervous system begin to develop only a few weeks after conception. The cells forming the new little person begin to separate into different structures. A layer of cells called the ectoderm releases some of those cells to form the neural plate from which the brain and nervous system will develop.

A protein called Neural Growth Factor (NGF) begins to grow some of these cells into glial, the brain's glue. NGF receives its instructions from so-called regulatory genes and from chemical signals from nearby cells. As the embryo develops, first the nervous system forms the neural core. Then the neural plate curls into the neural tube, which in turn develops into the brain, the spinal cord and the complete nervous system. In the embryo, approximately 250,000 neurons will be generated every minute for the next nine months. The primary brain-building tasks are completed in the fetus by about four and a half months.

This brain development in the four and a half-month-old child is equivalent to wiring a large city for communication. By birth, all the systems have been checked and re-checked. Neurons are firing if all is well. Since areas of the brain use high sugar levels as they develop, localized brain development in a child is tracked by measuring glucose levels. Positron Emission Tomography (PET) is used to measure the glucose levels. During this process, the person is injected with radioactive glucose, which mixes with blood and goes to the brain. The more active a part of the brain, the more glucose it uses. PET sensors locate the source of the heightened glucose usage and feed the information into computers that then show the "hot spots" of increased activity.

PETs, CAT scans, MRIs and SQUIDs are all technologies developed by the mind to study itself and the brain. Computer Assisted Tomography (CAT) produces pictures of the brain's structure but does not distinguish between dead or live brain cells. Magnetic Resonance Imaging (MRI) generates detailed pictures of the brain but cannot detect brain function. Superconductivity Quantum Interference Device (SQUID) detects brain activity by picking up magnetic fields. Firing neurons create electric current. Electric fields induce magnetic fields, which when detected by the SQUID indicate brain activity.

Man is the only being created who has the intelligence and ability to generate tools that he uses to study himself. This intelligence is obvious at birth. Though it is not etched in stone, neuroscientists say our brains finish creating neurons by age five. The brain of a four-year-old is twice as metabolically active as that of an adult. This is true until about age ten, then the brain tapers off at adult levels by age sixteen. This means that one of greatest windows of learning opportunity occurs during the childhood years up to about age ten. Music is one area where this has proved to be true. More than ninety percent of the children in America having perfect musical pitch began studying music by age four.

Our dancing minds are amazingly supple and capable of much more complex tasks than they are usually given. The mind, like the brain, is capable of astonishing feats well into old age. Einstein is a perfect example. At age seventy-six, he was still working on the physics that perplexed him all his adult life. Dr. Marian Diamond found out why. When she examined Einstein's brain, there was remarkably little lipofuscin, or pigment in the neurons. Lipofuscin shows wear and tear on brain cells, and there was no trace of Alzheimer's.

Psychologist Mihaly Czikszentmihalyi (chick-sent-me-high) in his book Flow says our best moments occur when our bodies or minds are stretched to their limits "in a voluntary effort to accomplish something difficult." What causes a Newton, Carver, Einstein, Woods or Faraday to wrestle with complex scientific problems to which they themselves may never find answers? It is the thrill of the chase, in part. It is the fire inside. It is unanswered questions, unresolved problems, unrelenting challenges. What makes the great writer grapple with the nuances of plot, character and story? What makes the great general or politician master the art of war or statecraft? Why does a child become a tinkerer and later an inventor? Why does a child go from a street-corner lemonade merchant to an entrepreneur? It is the fire inside.

Inside you and me is a burning drive to achieve something significant. Some call this drive ambition. According to Gilbert Brim, we have a basic drive for growth and mastery that expresses itself in a variety of ambitions. Brim says we all want to be challenged and that when life becomes too easy, we create new challenges and place greater demands upon ourselves. He also says when we perceive life to be too hard, we adjust backward to ease some of the difficulty. We all want to participate in enterprises that are either cooperative or competitive, selfish or unselfish. We need dreams, visions, aspirations, desires, hopes and unselfish cooperative enterprises. This is the stuff of life; it is what keeps us alive; it is the fire inside.

Author Joseph Epstein calls ambition the secret passion. He writes with that passion.

> Ambition is one of the great transformers of human personality—a shaping force par excellence of human character. To have ambition or to be without it affects a person's conduct in every regard... Can a person learn more by testing himself, through ambition, against the world and only by reaching for his highest limits acquire knowledge of his depths? Or is it only by renouncing ambition, by living within oneself, that true selfknowledge is available? (Epstein, Elephant Paperbacks, 1980)

By ambition I do not mean the selfish thirst for blind indulgence, stepping on whomever necessary to get to the top. I do mean principled or Godly ambition. This ambition seeks the will of God. It is actively concerned with the circumstances of others. However, it refuses to make excuses or acknowledge phantom barriers to successfully reaching the goal. This ambition will never bury dreams or defer hope. This Godly ambition seeks to lift people to their maximum potential, then exult in the joy of seeing God's will fulfilled.

The playing of a violin concerto. The splitting of the atom. Hitting a golf ball perfectly straight down the fairway.

These are all largely functions of the mind. From the building of the pyramids of Egypt to the obelisk of London, man has used the powers of the mind to dream, envision, plan and build. What constitutes the mind of a builder, maker, master, artist or influencer? What mental characteristics are related to extraordinary achievement?

One of the most essential elements in extraordinary achievement is getting a head start. Becoming positively exposed to one's lifetime passion at age three or four gives a person an advantage of developing the multiple skills needed to master a domain. (Read more on this topic in Chapter 4, titled The World of the Child.) In addition, neurologist and educator Howard Gardner notes three characteristics of extraordinary achievers:

1) They reflect on both the large and small events of their lives.

2) They are less distinguished by their raw powers than by an enormous ability to identify and exploit their strengths.

3) They fail often and dramatically. However, they do not quit. Instead they learn from their setbacks and convert defeats into opportunities.

While passion will get you moving, it is not enough to carry you through the length of the journey. How many people do you know who started out with what might have been a brilliant idea and had simply passion to go along with the idea. We need passion, and lots of it. But we also need process. Process is the how-to. How am I going to get this thing done? How will I get this product to market? How will I get the training I need to become a physicist or biologist? Where is my greatest opportunity for achievement? What are my strengths and weaknesses? How will I get this song recorded or this proposal submitted?

You have not begun to exhaust your intellectual and creative powers. Jesus said that with faith we can move mountains and realize the impossible. What Godly thing can your mind begin to conceive for you to accomplish? What can you focus on like a laser with your God-given mental powers? Maybe it's a new career. Perhaps you are in a profession that was not your first choice, but you went into it because the academic preparation was easier. Now you are bored and envious of those who persevered in that field. You may begrudge their achievements, even though you really are not that kind of person.

If this is you, it is not too late for you to fulfill the purpose of God for your life. Every person has within them a burning fire to achieve something. And God has given you a mind with amazing powers. You don't have to see yourself as an intellectual—you can develop to an extraordinary degree the powers that God has given you.

To achieve the extraordinary, you will need to be competent in a specific domain. Being competent means having the acquired skills and habits that result from refining and perfecting native abilities. Nobel laureate Herbert Simon and his colleagues have done research on competence. They have discovered that since man is a symbol processing being, very competent people are those who have learned to process the greatest number of symbols and patterns. By symbols, Simon means things such as the letters in an alphabet, the pieces on a chess board, the dots and dashes in Morse Code and so on. Competent people are those who know and/or do something well. On the extreme, an expert is said to have tens of thousands of "knowledge chunks" in memory.

This may take time. Researcher John Hayes says no one reaches world class in any field in less than ten years. I will substitute "Kingdom Class" for world class, meaning that standard of excellence less than which is never expected of citizens of the Kingdom of God. Length of time to achieve was also the topic of a study conducted at the University of Chicago by Benjamin Bloom and his associates. The study, called the Development of Talent Project, examined the careers of extraordinary concert pianists, sculptors, research mathematicians, research neurologists, Olympic swimmers and tennis champions.

Twenty-four concert pianists were examined and revealed that on average, it took them 17.14 years from their first lesson to the time when they won a major international competition. The mathematicians and neurologists required even more time to develop mastery in their domain. The extraordinary tennis players often had begun to play by age three or four. All of these individuals possessed a laser-like focus on the task at hand.

Many people do not seem to understand that regardless of whatever inherited mental or physical abilities one may have, behavior is a critical factor in determining the person's future. All the research points to the fact that practice is essential in extraordinary achievement. This is not just related to motor function. The pianist may practice scales in his or her imagination while lying in bed at night. This is as valuable to the development of virtuosity as the literal playing of the scales.

As a child, physicist Richard Feynman labored hours over mathematical calculations. It is exciting news that intellectual capacities may be significantly enhanced. With practice, you may improve your memory, computational skills, conceptional thinking, verbal skills, visual thinking, associative learning and so on. There is dormant mind power in you. But perhaps misconceptions about the nature of intelligence and your own intellectual capacities have disempowered you. When you realize this and begin to apply certain strategies for mental growth, you will be astonished. God gave you a mind that rises to mental challenges.

Shinichi Suzuki, pioneer of the famed Suzuki Method of violin instruction, says: "Ability is life. ... Man is governed by the life force. The living soul, with the desire to go on living, displays great power in adapting itself to its environment. The human life force, by seeing and feeling its surroundings, trains itself and develops ability. This ability by further constant training overcomes difficulties and becomes very high ability. This is the relationship between a human being and ability. The development of ability cannot be accomplished by mere thinking or theorizing, but must be accompanied by action and practice."

I share Suzuki's belief that it is foolish to lament lack of talent. God has placed within every person the capacity to do something very well. How committed you are to practice that will determine how accomplished you become. Most of us do not like the methodical approach to developing the kind of competency that leads to extraordinary achievement, but there is no other way.

Washington Irving said, "Great minds have purposes; others have wishes." Bessie Coleman, "Queen Bess," was one person who had a purpose. She surpassed all the obstacles to become the first black American to earn an international pilot's license. While working in the cotton fields of Texas and later in a beauty parlor in Chicago, Queen Bess had a vision of herself flying. Because no flight school in America would accept a black woman at the time, Queen Bess went to France, where she was licensed two years before Amelia Earhart by the reputable Federation Aeronautique Internationale. Proverbs 23:7 states that as a man thinketh in his heart (mind), so is he.

One of the great mistakes made in charismatic and Pentecostal churches is the negligence regarding the development of the extent of the mind's powers for use in the service of Almighty God.

Many people have been discouraged by a report that they or their children have received concerning a "learning difficulty." The reading difficulty dyslexia, attention deficit disorder (ADD), dyscalculia (difficulty calculating) and dysorthography (difficulty spelling) have held many people from striving to achieve their potential. Did you know that both Einstein and Picasso were dyslexic? Also, according to Edison biographer Neil Baldwin, young Thomas, or Al as he was called, was "inattentive, dreamy, distracted, drifted off during recitations, and drew and doodled in his notebook instead of repeating rote lessons."

Edison, who did not even start school until he was eight years old, dropped out after only three months. However, this precocious young man had his own laboratory at age ten, and by age twelve, he had his own business selling food on the railroad. One of the things marking Einstein, Edison, G.W. Carver and all extraordinary achievers is a voracious appetite for reading. By age ten, Edison had read every book in the public library in his home town. During the mid-1880s, when he lived in Llewellyn Park, New Jersey, he kept a running tab at Brentano's bookstore in Manhattan. It was not unusual for Edison to order hundreds of dollars in books every month. He would read every available book and periodical on any subject that caught his interest.

Another extraordinary achiever, Albert Einstein, did not speak until late and then with some difficulty. But he began to tap the powers of his mind at an early age. At age five, sick and in bed, Einstein became intrigued by the mysterious force that caused the needle on a compass to point north. He wrestled with trying to figure out how it worked. Pauline Einstein tutored her young charge at home until he was seven. He did not enter elementary school until age nine, then his teachers resurrected early fears that he was retarded. Einstein showed no interest in sports, he behaved strangely, and he failed to benefit at all from the rote methods of the classroom. He stubbornly ignored anything that bored him, but intractably committed to whatever caught his interest.

Einstein biographer Ronald Clark writes that Einstein was expelled from the Munich gymnasium (college preparatory school) for being disruptive. When his father, Hermann, went to the school and inquired about what profession young Albert was suited for, the headmaster told him that it did not matter, for young Albert "would never amount to anything."

Michael Faraday, the scientist who discovered lines of electromagnetic force and electromagnetic induction, left school at age thirteen. Taking a job as the errand boy for a bookbinder, Faraday read through the entire Encyclopedia Britannica, keeping a notebook of questions and quotations generated by his reading. Electromagnetic induction says that electric current can be produced by thrusting a magnet into a coil of wire and withdrawing it. By giving birth to the transformer and the dynamo, Faraday extended the domain of electricity. His major research was done in his basement. Mind you, Faraday made his discoveries in electromagnetic induction while being, in the words of Isaac Asimov, "completely innocent of mathematics."

Faraday manifested learning difficulties. He had early problems with speech, spelling and an unreliable memory. However, because of a strong visual acuity and a potent imagination, he overcame his setbacks.

As these three men prove, so-called learning difficulties do not have to arrest your potential. Learning difficulties are often the converse of giftedness or prodigy. Even people diagnosed as autistic may demonstrate profound numeracy. There are those who have suffered serious head injuries which triggered prodigious artistic abilities not evidenced before the accident.

Although Einstein was worth only sixty-five thousand dollars when he died, his contributions to the domain of physics are unquestioned. Over six decades, Edison registered more than one thousand patents, and it is said that business interests based on or largely due to Edison's inventions amounted to more than twenty-five billion dollars.

Another over-achiever, retired basketball all-star and warrior athlete Michael Jordan, has an unquenchable fire inside. Jordan possesses an indomitable will to win, along with what is to some an intimidating work ethic. He seems to thrive on the pressure that most mortals avoid at all costs. Jordan has passion, intensity and prolonged focus. Another athlete, legendary NFL receiver Jerry Rice, is a future Hall of Fame inductee. His work ethic has become the stuff of which legends are made. Even though Rice and Jordan have achieved every conceivable individual and team accolade in their respective sports, they continued to drive themselves like rookies hungry to prove themselves to the world.

The fire inside does not respect domains. The fire inside is about what Abraham Maslow called the need for self-actualization. Maslow says that unless a person is doing what he or she is individually fitted for, a discontent and restlessness will develop. He says musicians must make music, artists must paint, and poets must write if they ever are to be at peace with themselves. Maslow says that what people can be they must be. People must be true to themselves.

This is a biblical concept. Proverbs 13:12 says,

"Delayed hope makes one sick at heart, but a fulfilled longing is a tree of life" (God's Word).

This concept is reiterated in Verse 19, which says, "A fulfilled desire is sweet to the soul."

A desire in Hebrew means a longing, delight, charm or satisfaction, something wished or coveted after. The biblical Hebrew definition of fulfill or accomplish is to have breath, to be, to exist. The word sweet in this second verse means giving security.

God has planted a desire, a fire, inside you. He has planted a delight, a charm, inside you. Until you accomplish it, you will not have the true security of being that only God can give. God gave you powers of mind to help you fulfill the longing within you. But you must harness your power of thought and commit to the purpose of God. You do not have the luxury of being an undisciplined thinker. Your mind needs thought to serve you. Right thinking helps you cultivate and use your vast God-given mental powers.

Just ask author and speaker Glenn Bland, who says: "People who fail to devote adequate time to the business of thinking fall woefully short of reaching their potential... A definite purpose, conceived through productive thought, creates energy capable of uncommon accomplishment." This applied to Einstein. He valued his imagination above knowledge.

Exactly what are thoughts? One of the Hebrew words for thought is chashab (khaw-shab). It means to interpenetrate, weave or fabricate; mental effort, regard, value, compute, conceive, make account of, devise, esteem, imagine, find out, forecast, impute, invent, be like, purpose, reckon, regard. Thoughts in the Bible also mean plans, intentions and work.

The Bible is unsurpassed in its wisdom for the optimum development of the mind. In Romans 12:2, the apostle Paul tells us to "renew" our minds. Renew here means to renovate. It connotes to make fresh and youthful, to regenerate. It involves repetition, reversal and intensity. Renewing the mind means that through repetition and intensity, we train our minds to conceive and produce after the perfect will of God.

You must understand that the majority of your limitations are self-imposed.

We are capable of understanding all the laws of God, including those that allow the development of technology and the continuation of invention. Our minds are capable of understanding machines This means we can master levers, block and tackle, wheels and axles, incline planes and wedges, screws, gears, work, force, power, pressure, hydrostatics, hydraulics, complex machines and internal combustion engines. We can learn mathematics, physics, astronomy, aerodynamics and music. We can learn differentials, mechanical multipliers and integrators. God equipped us to do all these things if we ignite the fire inside.

Ronald Erwin McNair had a fire inside. Born to a poor family in racially segregated Lake City, South Carolina, he dreamed of physics, of flying and of some day becoming America's first black astronaut. Nothing could delay his hope, not even the virulent racism he encountered constantly. In high school, McNair became an honor student, a decorated

Scout, an accomplished athlete, a skillful musician, a karate champion and class valedictorian. After graduating magna cum laude from North Carolina Agricultural and Technical University, he attended the Massachusetts Institute of Technology, where he earned a doctorate in physics. McNair performed some of the first experiments with high-pressure lasers at MIT. He joined NASA in 1978 and made his first flight into space in 1984. He was killed on January 28, 1986, along with six other heroic Americans, when the space shuttle Challenger exploded. The fire inside Dr. McNair made him an extraordinary achiever in life and a true hero after his death.

Ronald McNair had a hunger for knowledge since he was a young boy. He read every book his family bought, then borrowed more from neighbors. Still his appetite for knowledge was not satisfied. At age nine, a determined Ronald dared enter Lake City's "For Whites Only" public library and refused to leave. The police were called, as were Ronald's parents, Carl and Pearl McNair. Ronald was found sitting on a desk holding a pile of books on his lap. His calm, non-disruptive manner assured the librarian and the police that all he wanted was the books. From that moment, Ronald was allowed to check out all the books he wanted.

Do you possess this kind of hunger for knowledge? Do you have this kind of drive to learn? This is a part of the mindset of the extraordinary achiever. Every extraordinary achiever I have studied was almost consumed with the passion to know and understand things. These people are not satisfied with a superficial understanding of things. They must know in depth.

Perhaps you have heard of Benjamin Banneker, another extraordinary achiever. He was a great mathematician and surveyor. Banneker was appointed by President George Washington in 1791 to design the District of Columbia. This was the first time a black American had received a presidential appointment. As a boy, Banneker was obsessed with reading. He chose to read books rather than play with other children. While still fairly young, Banneker was given a pocket watch by traveling salesman Josef Levi. The watch intrigued Banneker. He disassembled and reassembled it many times, studying the gears and movements. In 1752, Banneker built his own clock using the pocket watch as his guide. Gathering parts from wherever he could find them, Banneker hand-carved every part of his clock. Every gear, chime and movement were meticulously hand-carved. His clock lasted for forty years.

Banneker had a reputation for sleeping late into the day, causing some to dismiss him as lazy. However, he slept late because he usually stayed awake into the early morning hours staring at the stars. He made maps of the stars and planets, and worked producing an almanac, which he published in 1792. Banneker accurately predicted a solar eclipse for April 4, 1789. His prediction went against predictions by many recognized astronomers and mathematicians of the day.

Edison, Einstein, Faraday, McNair and Banneker all were obsessed with learning and understanding. Many of the world's great achievers educated themselves into genius. A fire discovered inside them early was fueled throughout their lives by their relentless pursuit of knowledge. No book or journal was published in their field of interest without their knowing about it. No new research was conducted, no new discoveries were made, no new practitioners emerged without their knowing.

Much of contemporary Christianity has de-emphasized the life of the mind. Somehow passionate commitment to the highest development of our God-given mental faculties is seen as undesirable inasmuch as it's viewed simultaneously to be detrimental to the development of the spiritual powers. This false split-world view has placed the church on the fringes of the modern intellectual world. Evangelical professor Mark Noll once wrote:

> Evangelicals sponsor dozens of theological seminaries, scores of colleges, hundreds of radio stations and thousands of unbelievably diverse parachurch agencies—but not a single research university or a single periodical devoted to in-depth interaction with modern culture. (Mark A. Noll, Eerdmans, 1994)

How does the church expect to substantially influence secular culture when there is no peculiarly Christian voice in areas of public discourse? If there is a conspicuous "Scandal of the Evangelical Mind," what in God's name is going in charismatic and Pentecostal churches? With some exceptions, charismatic and Pentecostal conferences are given to emotionalism and shallow hype. African American are invited on Christian television to discuss racial issues. Almost never do we see them when there has been a new development in the sciences, or to discuss the relative merits of compassionate capitalism.

Even many Christian schools are wide of the mark. Thank God for the pastors who understand how valuable technical literacy is to the future and are building technical components into their schools. In just about every job, knowledge is doubling every two to three years. Just to stay current, employees will need to match that. People who do not continuously and fervently upgrade their skills will not remain current. People must be taught to value change and growth, and to mine the vast resources of their God-given mental powers.

Perhaps it will help put this into perspective by noting that between 1981 and 1991, one million manufacturing jobs disappeared. And only about seventeen percent of the United States workforce is blue-collar. While computers are doing a lot of work for people, the machines will never completely replace us. We must understand the skills we need to compete in the global economy. It is essential to learn to become part of a team. To this team you must bring highly developed technical and interpersonal skills. Approximately eighty percent of your success in the marketplace will be related to your interpersonal skills, and twenty percent to your technical skills. Do not be deceived by these percentages. The twenty percent that comprises your technical expertise must be honed sharply. You will have no choice but to become a lifelong learner. As you understand and walk in covenant with God, your greatest source of wealth for the future will be His covenant promises and the tremendous brain-mind power He has given you to generate new ideas and solutions to problems.

It is said that fast thinking and clear thinking are essential personal skills for the twenty-first century. Possessing these skills will better enable you to rely on yourself in the economy. Self-reliance allows you to manage your learning, to understand the value of information, and to possess the wisdom to use that information to develop products and services of use to our world. The home, church and school all must become master learning environments. As much emphasis must be given to the development of the mind as to that of the spirit.

Excited, incinerated minds must be encouraged and nurtured. There are those who are called to live on the edge. They are summoned by God to be risk-takers. They are the passionate learners and doers. But God calls all His people to be doers, or performers. You have an innovative, creative mind. Sometimes, as in the case of Einstein, Edison and Banneker, the world of an innovator or creative person is a lonely one. You may spend seasons reading, learning and preparing for the contribution that God has preordained for you to make.

The Catholic church ostracized Galileo for his telescope. The same treatment was given to Guttenburg for his printing press. Columbus was imprisoned. Newton and Pasteur were ridiculed. No one paid much attention to the discoveries of Copernicus during his lifetime.

Despite this, when God gives you an idea, you must be willing to bet the farm on it. You must be prepared to endure ostracism, ridicule or even something worse. You may have to buck against the existing paradigm in your industry or field.

You must be prepared to allow your intellect, ego, reputation, family, competence and sanity to be attacked. On top of it all, you may be wrong. However, you may be right, and you will never know until you risk it all. This is the stuff that life is made of. The great adventure, filled with tremendous risks and incredible opportunities. Risk-taking is a key ingredient to success in any enterprise.

The search for new discoveries almost always will place you on the fringes of your domain. Innovation almost never comes from the center; it comes from the edges, from those who dare to think in bold, iconoclastic ways. Do not be afraid to allow your interests to roam the field on which you are trained for associations, metaphors, connections and so on. Gregor Mendel was a minister when he discovered the foundational concepts for the science of genetics. Galileo had his training in medicine—not in astronomy and science where he made the discoveries for which we remember him. Luigi Galvani, whose research on the manner in which nerves and muscles conduct electricity became the basis for the invention of the electric battery, also had been trained in medicine—not in electricity.

American schools—public or private, secular or church—do not favor the dancing mind. In an attempt to teach respect for the canons of traditional knowledge, discipline, order, punctuality and so on, our creative powers are generally ignored. Curiosity and experimentation die in most of us at an early age. Unless you were blessed with exceptional parents or with a significant other who will not allow your fire to go out, you may have lost your sense of childlike wonder and enthusiasm long ago.

If this has happened to you, you can get it back. Begin to indulge your interests. Challenge your mind to learn new things, to solve problems varying in complexity. Yours is a dancing mind. It does not suffer your being a wallflower gladly. Come alive with intrigue over the created universe of Almighty God.

Remember, beyond your psychological, safety, love and esteem needs lies a need for self-actualization. The Bible says that fulfilled longings give us breath, or life. To delay the fulfillment of your God-given dream will depress you. It will fill you with anxiety, which has been defined as the tension of being against non-being. In other words, it is the struggle with knowing that what you are is nowhere near what you could be. It is the struggle with knowing that what you are doing is nowhere near what you could be doing. This drains your energy and robs you of your zest for life. Most importantly, it is not God's plan for you.

Your mind is endowed by God with enormous conceptual, creative, analytical, mathematical, language and reasoning powers. They must be trained and put to use in the service of God and man.

The Bible says that as a man thinketh in his heart (mind), so is he. If you have told yourself that you cannot learn a certain subject, or master certain symbols, you generally are wrong. Your thoughts on this matter, however, keep you from putting forth the effort that is necessary to master any new domain of knowledge.

There are many books on the functions and power of the mind. A trip to your local library or bookstore, or a search on the Internet will put you on the path to learning more about the mental capabilities that God has given you.

3

INTELLIGENCE

Your wonderfully crafted and powerful mind possesses a high degree of intelligence. Intelligence is defined as the ability to solve the problems one encounters in life, the ability to generate new problems to solve, and the ability to make a product or offer a service that is valued in one's culture. Before the pioneering work of Harvard and Project Zero's Howard Gardner, we held a view of intelligence that was generated by the work of Lewis Terman at Stanford in the early 1920s.

Terman set out to identify the specific traits of children with high IQs, then to track their lives to see what became of them. He studied fifteen hundred children born between 1903 and 1917. Terman was seeking to demonstrate that children gifted academically would also prove to be gifted socially and athletically. Terman sought to disprove the notion that academic achievers were socially inept and athletically pathetic. Terman also believed that a high IQ in a hild was a predictor of what the child would achieve as an adult.

Terman's sample group was disproportionately male and middle class. Thirty-three percent of the participants in the study came from middle-class families, which at the time constituted only about three percent of the United States population. Participants in Terman's study were nominated by their teachers based on their perception of the children's ability. Teachers were to choose the youngest and most able students in their classes. These students were given a preliminary test. Those who scored 135 or higher then were given a complete test. As you can see, the study was not conducted on a random sample of children. Therefore, when evaluating the results of Terman's studies, one has to factor in the variables. It is also important to note that the children in the study were caucasian.

Later Terman modified a test by another IQ tester, Alfred Binet. This test has come to be known as the Stanford-Binet test. It measures language, logic, math and spatial ability. An average score on the Stanford-Binet test is in the ninety to 109 range, where approximately fifty percent of the people tested fall. Only two or three out of every one hundred students have IQs of one hundred thirty or higher, and only about one in one hundred has an IQ of one hundred forty or more. About one person in ten thousand to thirty thousand has an IQ of one hundred sixty or more, and about one in a million score one hundred eighty or more. With the exception of physics, where the average doctorate-degree holder has an IQ of one hundred forty, the average doctorate-degree holder in the United States has a score of one hundred thirty.

If you find these statistics dizzying, do not worry. Reliable research has confirmed no constant correlation between IQ and achievement. In fact, we are told that when an IQ reaches a certain point, say one hundred thirty, it can become an obstacle to success. The teachers in Terman's study chose students with their own biases, as we all would have done. However, this is not to suggest the students who were not chosen may not have possessed abilities superior to those chosen for the study. At certain points in their lives, certainly neither Einstein nor Edison would have been chosen for such a study.

Today all sorts of fascinating research is available concerning human intelligence. It is imperative to study this research. Many people have children diagnosed with learning disabilities and placed in remedial situations and/or put on prescription drugs. In many cases, the parents are made to believe that their child cannot learn. Perhaps the child scored poorly on an IQ test. It is important to remember that IQ tests are not precise measurements. They limited measure performance, not potential. Do not despair if your child scores poorly on one of these tests, and do not allow anyone to tell you your child cannot learn. The human brain and mind are created marvels of God.

Your child indeed may have a learning disability. However, this is not to be extrapolated across the range of the child's abilities. Many children with learning disabilities in one area possess genius in another area. The late physicist Richard Feynman had the lowest literature and history scores of any student ever admitted to graduate school at Princeton, where he was admitted in 1939. However, his math and physics scores were the highest the graduate admissions committee had ever seen. In fact, his physics score was perfect. It is not uncommon for those who are gifted in a specific area to be uninterested in other areas. In addition, it is not uncommon for children showing genius in an area to be learning-disabled in other areas.

The Bible stresses the importance of pursuing knowledge to gain intelligence. The prophet Hosea laments:

> My people are destroyed for lack of knowledge: because thou hast rejected knowledge, I will also reject thee, that thou shalt be no priest to me: seeing thou hast forgotten the law of thy God, I will also forget thy children (Hosea 4:6, KJV).

The Hebrew word for knowledge here is daath (dah-ath). It is cross-referenced to yada (yaw-daw), meaning intelligence, skill gained by instruction, observation, diligence. It means people who are cunning, discerning, discovering, comprehending, inventive, possessing skill. It means to give, have or take knowledge, to have great understanding, to teach, to be learned, to have opinions. The Hebrew word mada (mad-daw) specifically means intelligence and intelligent thought.

Almighty God says in this verse that the lack of intelligence is consequential. The old saying "What you don't know won't hurt you" couldn't be more wrong. God says the ignorant are destroyed. Destroyed in Hosea's passage means literally dumb or silent; brought to silence, utterly undone; cut down or off. The word "lack" in "lack of knowledge" means failure, destruction, being without.

God says where His people have not intelligence they are made to be dumb. They cannot speak; they are undone, brought to naught, cut down, mired in failure and without. This is not the state God desires for His people. Remember, intelligence is defined as the ability to solve problems. You and I were created to be problem-solvers. God intends for us, under His authority, to develop our intelligence, which He gave us, to a high problem-solving level.

The biblical prophet Daniel was an intelligent problem-solver. God strategically placed Daniel in the kingdom of Babylon. Daniel, whose name means "he who delivers judgment in the name of God", was a scholar whose heart was right with God. Daniel 1:4b says Daniel was:

- "trained in every kind of wisdom, well-informed, quick at learning" (Jerusalem Bible).

- "skilled in all branches of learning, equipped with knowledge, and endowed with intelligence" (American Translation).

- "at home in all branches of knowledge, well-informed, intelligent" (New English Bible).

- "competent to serve in the king's palace"

(Revised Standard Version).

In fact, Daniel 1:20 says Daniel and his colleagues were ten times as knowledgeable as the Babylonian magicians and astrologers.

> On all subjects in which grasp and information counted, the king, as he questioned them, found

them ten times more able than all the magicians
and astrologers in his entire realm –("Berkeley
Translation).

Never a question the king could propound, to
make trial of their learning and quick wits, but
they could answer it ten times better than any
diviner or sage in his kingdom –(Knox Translation)

The intelligence of Daniel, Hananiah, Mishael and
Azariah positioned them close to a king who had a problem
to which none of his problem-solvers had a solution. The
problem so vexed the king that he issued a decree to take the
lives of those magicians and astrologers who had reached
their limits. The onset of the Peter Principle forced these men
to plan their funerals. God gave the man of God, Daniel, the
solution to the king's problem, the interpretation of his
dream, and spared the lives of the magicians and astrologers.
In the process, God caused Nebuchadnezzar to bestow favor
upon Daniel and promoted him to president.

(Daniel 2:48 says the king "raised Daniel to high rank,
and showered riches on him" (The Know). All this was
because Daniel took seriously the disciplined development of
his God-given gifts and became a problem-solver. All over
the world, there are problems to be solved. There are problems in biology, physics, media, communications, medicine,
literature, astronomy, mathematics, law, ethics, sociology, psychology, philosophy, geo-politics, the military, government,
economics, travel, art, music, business, theology, anthropology, education, employment, foreign and domestic policy, lead-

ership, national morale and so on. On which of these problems are you training to have an impact?

Haward Gardner, a Harvard neurologist, has postulated the existence of at least seven kinds of intelligence. As opposed to the "psychometric" (Determined by IQ tests) view of intelligence posited by Terman, Gardner suggests the existence of intelligences not measurable in the main by IQ tests. The existence of multiple intelligences implies multiple learning styles.

Gardner shares my belief that IQ tests do not measure potential. He writes, "Moreover, the intelligence test reveals little about an individual's potential for further growth." Gardner then quotes the famous Russian psychologist Vygotsky, who stated, "intelligence tests fail to yield any indication of an individual's zone of potential, or proximal development."

Gardner identifies these seven types of intelligences:

1) Linguistic intelligence—the ability to think in words and to use language to express and appreciate complex meanings. This intelligence is usually manifested in authors, print and broadcast journalists and professional speakers, among others.

2) Logical/mathematical intelligence—the ability to calculate, quantify, consider propositions and hypotheses, and carry out complex mathematical operations. Scientists, engineers, mathematicians, accountants and computer programmers all manifest this intelligence.

3) Bodily/kinesthetic intelligence—an ability to manipulate objects and to highly develop physical skills. Athletes, dancers, surgeons and craftsmen are examples of people with this intelligence.

4) Musical intelligence—Those demonstrating particular sensitivity to pitch, melody, rhythm and tone probably possess this intelligence. It would be evident in composers, conductors, musicians, instrument makers, singers and so on.

5) Interpersonal intelligence—an ability to understand and work effectively with others. Teachers, pastors, social workers and civil servants perhaps would manifest this intelligence.

6) Intrapersonal intelligence—the ability to realize an accurate perception of oneself and to use this knowledge in planning and living one's life. Pastors, teachers, philosophers and some counselors might be examples of this intelligence.

7) Spatial intelligence—the ability to think three- dimensionally, as do architects, pilots, sailors, sculptors and painters.

To Gardner's seven intelligences should be added at least these four:

1) Moral intelligence—the acknowledgment of and adherence to Biblical notions of right and wrong in all areas of endeavor, not excluding those wherein the seven intelligences are manifested.

2) Emotional intelligence—This has been defined by Daniel Goleman as the ability to motivate oneself and persist in the face of frustrations, to control impulse and delay gratification, to regulate one's moods and keep distress from swamping the ability to think, to empathize and hope.

3) Successful intelligence—This is defined by author Robert Sternberg as that which incorporates the analytical, the creative and the practical. He says successfully intelligent people have and use these three aspects of the mind. We use the analytical to solve problems and to judge the quality of ideas; the creative to generate new ideas and problems to solve; and the practical to implement new ideas and solutions in useful ways.

4) Spiritual intelligence—the humble acknowledgment of the existence of the God of the Bible as Creator and Sustainer of the universe, the Personal Uncaused Cause, and of His Son Jesus Christ, begotten of the Father, born of a virgin, God and man, Savior of the world, sovereign King and Potentate; the acknowledgment of the holy Scriptures as inspired, authoritative and infallible.

The ways in which you learn, visualize, approach problems, construct knowledge models and so on are keys to which of these intelligences is dominant in you. Gardner says most of us have more than one of these intelligences, although one probably will be more prominent. Do you know what your dominant intelligence is? What about that of your spouse or your children? If not, find out, then do all you can to develop your own to your maximum potential and encourage others to do the same. God Almighty expects us to develop and use every gift He has given us. Proverbs 22:29 (KJV) says: "Seest thou a man diligent in his business? he shall stand before kings; he shall not stand before mean men."

Diligent in this verse is from two Hebrew words: yada and sakal, both of which mean intelligence. Business literally means employment, deputyship or that over which one has been given ambassadorship. It connotes something to which one has been dispatched as a messenger. The notion of assignment is being taught here. The man in Proverbs 22:29 has an assignment from God.

Stand in that verse means to be placed or stationed; to continue to present oneself; to stand fast, stand forth, stand still, stand up; to speak surely. The man intelligent at his assignment shall be stationed in the presence of rulers. He shall go out among them, and his counsel shall be spoken surely.

Just as God has prepared an assignment for you, He has prepared people for you. The passionate pursuit of your assignment will bring you into the presence of the people to whom you have been assigned and who have been assigned to you.

What God has assigned you to is that for which He has gifted you. Your particular array of intelligences, the wisdom and knowledge you have by the grace of God, are all keys to why you are on this earth. In Luke 19:12, 13, Jesus uses a parable to teach His disciple a truth of the Kingdom. He says:

...A certain nobleman went into a far country to receive for himself a kingdom, and to return. And he called his ten servants, and delivered them ten pounds, and said unto them, Occupy till I come (KJV).

Before the nobleman in the parable (Christ Himself) demanded anything of his servants, He gave them something to invest. According to Gerhard Kittel's Theological Dictionary of the New Testament, the Greek word for occupy, pragmateia, from which we get the English word pragmatic, means "zealous prosecution of or concern with a matter; work or the affairs of men; business, or something with which one is occupied; affairs of state; official duties; mental work: treatise writing, especially works of history; a task to be carried out; to be a businessman; to compose; business as a means of livelihood; intellectual pursuits; to do business in trade or money lending; be a business partner; to deal with radically, investigate closely; render political service." According to Kittel, the pragmaton is one who seeks to "set secular society under the will of God."

As you can see, this is not a summons to mediocrity. Intelligence is a gift from God. He rewards the diligent cultivation and application of it. I meet so many people who are constrained by a limited perception of their abilities. Most people would do more than they are doing if they believed they could. Well, you can. You have not yet begun to place a demand upon the breadth of intelligence that God has given you.

Acts 1:8 says we shall receive power after the Holy Spirit has come upon us. This is a powerful verse; however, it usually is rendered exegetically incomplete. The Greek word for power is from the word group, dunamai, dunateo, dunatos, dunamis. We most often concern ourselves with the supernatural implications of the terms, as well we should. However, the word dunamis means more. It is borrowed by the Holy Spirit from the secular Greek for its multiple meanings. A person having a specific ability, capacity or power was referred to as dunatos. The word here means to be able or capable in a broad sense.

Dunamis was applied to the whole of life. It applied to the powers of hearing and sight, which were called dunameis. In addition, your moral, spiritual and intellectual powers are called dunameis. A person with no ability was called adunatos. The "a" before the word in Greek, called the alpha privative, negates the meaning of whatever follows.

Dunasteis is a person who can do something, who has the sense of power, might and dominion. The word was used for human rulers and literally means to be endued with the strength of Yahweh. You are a dunasteis. You are endued with the strength of Yahweh. The ability that God gives at salvation permeates your entire being. He supernaturally floods you with ability in your body, intellect, emotions and so on. You have the touch of God on whatever intelligences you have. Whatever intelligences, gifts and abilities have always been in you now have the touch of God upon them. This places a greater responsibility upon you to develop them to the highest degree possible. You are a problem-solver!

That may come as a shock to you. When you find that fire inside, when you discover your intelligences, gifts and abilities, you will thrive on developing them. Even when it is hard and you have to push yourself to the next level, you will love every moment of it. You may say to yourself, "This is lonely, and all this practice, all this research, all this study, prayer and preparation are so hard." Then you will smile and go on. You'll enjoy every hardship and every task. You'll sleep better at night and awaken refreshed. You will feel the growth inside. Give God praise! He is working in you, causing you to desire and perform His will for your life.

Furthermore, in Acts 1:8, the word translated "receive" as it relates to power is lambano in Greek. It means to take or seize, ability in this case. As you seize or develop the ability God has placed in you, you will need bigger challenges. Your skills always will demand challenges equal to them.

In Matthew 25: 14, 15, Jesus teaches us more on the subject of responsibility for abilities:

> For the kingdom of heaven is as a man travelling
> into a far country, who called his own servants,
> and delivered unto them his goods. And unto one he
> gave five talents, to another two, and to another
> one; to every man according to his several ability;
> and straightway took his journey (KJV).

Ability here is the same word as power in Acts 1:8. Several in Matthew 25:15 is the Greek word idios, meaning that pertaining to the self; private, separate; thine own alone. It denotes those abilities that belong exclusively to you. Jesus distributed to them based on their individual abilities and expected results from them based on the same. Several abilities and multiple intelligences can be used interchangeably.

In the parable, Jesus expects His servants to use their unique abilities to solve the problem of increasing His capital. You know the story. Two of the servants solved the problem for Jesus and were promoted and given increased responsibility. The third, who solved no problem and blamed Jesus for expecting more from him than he was capable of delivering, had taken from him what he was originally given. Jesus expected competence. He expected these men to be skilled at their business. The one man who was not was banished from the presence of the Master.

While you serve God first and foremost through highly developed intelligences, you also serve man, society and culture. In Matthew 22, Jesus was questioned about the greatest commandment. In verse 37, He gives His response.

> "Master, which is the greatest commandment in
> the law?" Jesus said unto him, "Thou shalt love
> the Lord thy God with all thy heart, and with
> all thy soul, and with all thy mind."

The Greek word for mind here is dianoia (dee-an-oy-ah), meaning deep thought, the faculty or disposition of the mind; the exercise of the mind; the imagination and understanding. Dianoia is a compound composed of two words, dia, meaning channel, and nous, meaning intellect, place of knowledge and speech.

Repeatedly, the Bible says that the fear of the Lord is the beginning of knowledge and wisdom (Proverbs 1:7, 9:10). Fear means reverence or dread. The Hebrew word for beginning is rosh (roshe). It means the head; the most excellent or principal thing; the top, ruler, sum, chiefest thing; first in place, time, order or rank. The word techillah also is used for beginning. It means an opening, a commencement; something original, a first time. Therefore, the beginning of knowledge is the reverent worship of the one God Who reveals Himself in the Scriptures and in His creation. To exclude God from the training of the mind is to profane the whole of intellectual enterprise.

In the Jewish tradition, study and scholarship are considered forms of worship. It is absurd to think that the enterprise of scholarship may be carried out independent of the spiritual impulse. Man either worships God, himself or the creation. Intellectual pursuits that do not acknowledge God as the sovereign Creator of the universe are idolatrous. To not accept the limitations placed upon the mind of man by Almighty God is idolatrous.

The Jewish sage Moses Maimonides has given us great wisdom on this. In his Guide for the Perplexed, Maimonides writes:

> Know that for the human mind there are objects
> of perception which are within the scope of its
> nature and capacity; on the other hand, there
> are amongst things which actually exist, certain
> objects which the mind can in no way and by no
> means grasp: the gates of perception are closed
> against it. Further there are things of which
> the mind understands one part, but remains
> ignorant of the other; and when man is able to
> comprehend certain things, it does not follow that
> he must be able to comprehend everything...

A boundary is undoubtedly set to the human mind which it cannot pass. There are things (beyond that boundary) which are acknowledged to be in-accessible to human understanding, and a man does not show any desire to comprehend them, being aware that such knowledge is impossible, and that there are no means of overcoming the difficulty; e.g., we do not know the number of stars in heaven, whet-her the number is even or odd; we do not know the number of animals, minerals or plants.

By saying this, Maimonides is not suggesting that we not pursue the sciences. He simply is inoculating us against the expectation of being able to know everything. In fact, Maimonides says we should study everything within the scope of our intellectual powers. He says everyone possessing the talent and capacity for the higher methods of study based upon proof and rational argument should be advanced in the direction of perfection either by tutor or self-study.

The sciences in the culture of Maimonides were called the mysteries and the secrets of the law. The principles of the sciences were taught by wise men in riddles, as enigmas, shrouded in mysteries, so the student would be forced to tax himself mentally.

Maimonides offers a useful commentary on Proverbs 21:25, 26, which states:

The desire of the slothful killeth him; for his hands refuse to labor. He coveteth all the day long: but the righteous giveth and spareth not.

In these verses, Maimonides says Solomon "speaks of a man who desires to know the final results, but does not exert himself to understand the preliminary disciplines which lead to them, doing nothing else but desire... The majority of scholars, that is to say, the most famous in science, are afflicted with this failing, viz., that of hurrying at once to the final results, and of speaking about them, without treating the preliminary disciplines. Led by folly or ambition to disregard those preparatory studies, for the attainment of which they are either too incapable or too idle, some scholars endeavor to prove that these are injurious or superfluous. On reflection the truth will become obvious." According to this great Jewish sage, God has given us our intellects that we might grasp the essences of things.

To help put this into perspective, in the Greek world of Aristotle, the physical world consisted of substance, qualities, properties, form, accidents and essence. They were defined as follows:

> Substance—that part of an individual thing in which its properties inhere (what a thing is made of).

> Qualities—that by which we may identify an object, such as size, shape, color and weight.

> Properties—those qualities, including what an object does, that enable us to identify it.

> Form—what we can know and understand about the object.

> Accidents—those qualities not essential to the being of an object. In the case of a pencil, for example,

whether it was short or long, sharp or dull would be accident qualities.

Essence—the inner nature of a thing that is responsible for its qualities.

God has given us pour intellect to grasp the essences of things within the scope of our capacities. R.J. Rushdoony says in volume one of his Institutes of Biblical Law that, "Knowledge and science require a basis of law, fixity and pattern. Without this, there can be neither science or progress." God has given us an orderly cosmos, which by applying our mental powers we may investigate under His authority. No knowledge is purely the fruit of the investigative pursuits of man. All knowledge is revelational. It is either revelational through the Scriptures or through God's creation, which would be natural revelation. In other words, man may know nothing apart from that which God has revealed.

Epistemology, or the theory of knowledge, is the beginning of all intellectual pursuit. What we seek to know is truth. Truth is God's gift to man. This is the case whether man finds truth in a private and spiritual way, or whether he seeks truth concerning the atom and its properties.

In John's gospel, Jesus is referred to as the Logos. Logos is the underlying or unifying principle of a thing. Jesus Christ is the unifying field for which Einstein spent the last part of his life unsuccessfully searching. Logos also may translate to logic. Logic has been defined as the law of necessary inference. Jesus the Organizer, the Sustainer, of the universe makes intelligent logical discourse possible. Without Him there is no sensible conversation to be had. He is the Truth (John 14:6).

The Bible says that in Jesus Christ are hidden all the treasures of wisdom and knowledge (Colossians 2:3). Treasure in Greek is thesauros (thay-sow-rcs), also meaning a deposit or wealth. Jesus Christ is the treasure chest where the revelation for all twenty biblical words for wisdom and knowledge are locked up.

Hide in Colossians 2:3 means to conceal away fully, to keep a secret. We are not expected by God to begin the pursuit of knowledge by reciting the humanist credo. We enter the classroom, the laboratory, the workshop, the observatory and whatever experimental milieu, humbling ourselves before the Lord of all the earth, Jesus Christ. We seek revelation. We use the intelligence He has given us to the best of our abilities and expect results because the secret of the Lord is with them that fear Him.

The Fire Inside

4

The Genius Within Us

God has anointed your intellect, your intelligence. You have not given all you can give in the area where God has called you. What essences do you need God to reveal for you to make a tremendous breakthrough in your profession? You may be called by God to expand the domain of teaching or pathology. Maybe your seminal work is in astronomy or politics. Perhaps God wants to reveal to you the essence of mathematics from His perspective. The discovery of an elegant mathematical theorem given to you by the Spirit of God would allow you to minister to many in the scientific community.

Maybe God has called you to write great fiction. You may have started and thrown away the beginnings of a great novel. As an aspiring writer, God may want to give you subtleties of insight into the human psyche that will allow you to share Truth on another level.

Whatever you do or aspire to do, know that you are designed by God as an intelligent being. Discover your God-given talent, and cultivate and use it to the fullest extent. Never refer to yourself or anyone else as dumb. Your intelligence is far beyond what you have ever demanded of it. You choose to be an amateur, a specialist, an expert, a mastermind or a genius. In the case of genius, it is as much the fruit or perspiration as it is genetics. Remember, it is the man or woman skilled at his or her business whom God promises will stand before kings.

There is a fire of desire burning in your heart. In all probability, God has placed it there. You will never be happy or fulfilled until you respond to the fire. Your God-given intelligence is equivalent to the desire in your heart. It may need training, discipline and pushing, but it is there. Your unfulfilled childhood dreams still haunt you because they need to be fulfilled. They are not going to go away. It may be a long, slow road, but the alternative is you give up on life and live out the balance of your days with a sick heart. I know you do not want that. You must become like Jeremiah. You must become weary with postponing what God has placed in your heart.

Go to work today developing your intelligence(s). God has something significant He wants to reveal to you. Begin to expect it! Become excited about using your intelligence(s) to glorify God. Wherever you are, whatever you do, you are a potentially inestimable asset.

Knowing this demystifies genius for us. Usually when we think of genius, we imagine Einstein–the tossled hair, the pullover sweater or sweatshirt, pants not quite long enough and shoes but no socks. Stories of his so-called absentmindedness abound, as do stories of "the doctor," as he was reverently called by many, going out into bitter cold weather having forgotten his coat. Or we may think of Jerry Lewis' character in The Nutty Professor. We tend to think of the genius as being endowed with almost supernatural mental gifts but somehow being odd or strange. We justify his/her eccentricities by saying that the person thinks on a higher plane than we mere earthlings.

This is, for the most part, rubbish. There are traits of obsessiveness that may be associated with genius—this is what often gives birth to monumental achievement in the domain where the so-called genius works. However, there are traits of obsessiveness that tend to accompany extraordinary achievement in any area. Furthermore, according to the definition of genius, we are all capable of genius. The definition of genius is a person possessing a natural capacity of intellect, especially as shown in creative and original work in science, art, music and so on; natural capacity or talent, such as a genius for leadership; a distinct character or spirit as of a nation, period or language; a person who strongly influences for good or ill the character, conduct or destiny of a person, place or thing.

Certainly, we acknowledge that individuals are possessed of differing gifts, aptitudes, drives and applications.

However, it is practically undisputed that genius has as much to do with vision and work ethic as it does with genetics. It was the great inventor Thomas Alva Edison, a man with more than one thousand patents to his credit, who said genius is one percent inspiration and ninety-nine percent perspiration. The fact that the genius is an incredibly hard and tenacious worker is almost totally lost in our mythology. The fact that the genius may have worked on a particular problem all his or her adult life before discovering a breakthrough is also lost in our misperceptions. In the scientific community in particular, it is believed that a person is fortunate to gain a single meaningful insight in his or her career. More than one insight is thought to be an almost inexplicable gift.

This is a profound principle because the one discovery, whether it be in science, politics, medicine, economics, art or any other domain, may forever change the world. Usually those who change the world in any degree have diligently honed their gifts and have had historical circumstances thrust upon them.

Dr. Martin Luther King was a genius. The fact that history has labeled him a "civil rights leader" obscures the fact that Dr. King possessed one the finest analytical and philosophical minds America has ever produced. It is a crime of epic proportions to only acknowledge the oratorical genius of this great prophet of God. Dr. King's broad reading and learning stoked the fires of oratory refined and purified in the greatest tradition of black rhythmic ecclesiastical speech. He changed the nation and moved the world with his genius.

Dr. King, like most others who at some point in their lives are labeled genius, was a precocious child. By this I mean that at an earlier than average age, this person begins to take steps toward mastery in a particular area. It is usually an organized area of knowledge, such as mathematics, music, language, art, chess, gymnastics and so on. This child also progresses in the area or domain faster than others. This obviously has a lot to do with what the potentially precocious child is exposed to in his or her environment. The environment would include the people with whom the child comes in contact—their aspirations and expectations. It also would include the sensory richness or deprivation of the child's environment.

Harvard professor Dr. Ellen Winner has written that the gifted, or precocious, child also likes to march to his or her own drummer. By this she means the child needs little help from adults in the pursuit of mastery. The child is fueled by the excitement of his or her own discoveries, and this pushes the child to make even further discoveries. Dr. Winner points out that many times these gifted children devise novel ways of problem-solving and stretch the limits of the rules governing their particular domain.

Dr. Winner notes that these children are possessed of more than mere pedestrian interest in their domain. They have what she calls "a rage to master." They are obsessed with mastering the guardian rules of their chosen domain. Dr. Winner also describes the "child prodigy." This is the child who is so gifted that he or she performs at an adult level in the domain. Mozart and Beethoven would be examples of child-hood prodigies.

More structured, rule-governed domains such as math-ematics, music and chess tend to yield more identifiable gift-ed, prodigious children. This is because the rules reveal that which needs to be mastered and provides criteria for immedi-ate evaluation of performance and feedback. Children who may be gifted or prodigious in less rule-governed domains such as creative writing, visual arts or leadership may be hard-er to identify. However, their constant pushing of the enve-lope will eventually help to bring them notice.

All of us have the potential to excel in some specific domain. It is usually important to identify the domain early—though the rule is not hard and fast, as the lives of Einstein and Newton demonstrated. However, it seems as though there would be an obvious advantage to identifying and beginning early to master a specific domain.

I believe the church tends to de-emphasize the natural gifts and endowments placed in men by God. We should absolutely and with theological clarity teach the gifts of the Holy Spirit, but not to the neglect of God's so-called natural deposits in man.

> Every good gift and every perfect gift is from above, and cometh down from the Father of lights, with whom is no variableness, neither shadow of turning (James 1:17, KJV).

The Greek word for gift in this verse is the didomi (did-o-mee). It means adventure; bestow, bring forth, deliver, have power, minister, strike with the palm of the hand. This last definition connotes that to which you lay or put your hands to. The word good here means valuable or virtuous. Perfect is the Greek word teleios (tel-i-os). It means to complete in labor, growth, mental or moral character; to bring to completeness. It is interesting to note that in this word group is the word teleiosis (tel-i-o-sis), meaning completion, verification, performance, perfection of prophecy.

We know from the Bible that "gifts" may be imparted through prophecy.

> Neglect not the gift that is in thee, which was
> given thee by prophecy, with the laying on of hands
> of the presbytery (1 Timothy 4:14, KJV).

> This charge I commit unto thee, son Timothy,
> according to the prophecies which went before on
> thee, that thou mightest war a good warfare; Holding
> faith, and a good conscience (1 Timothy 1:18, 19a,
> KJV).

Conscience in the Greek means to see completely; to understand or become aware; to be informed of: consider, know, be privy of. The apostle Paul is reminding young Timothy of the prophetic words that had been spoken over him and the gift of God released thereby. He instructs Timothy to hold his faith with a good conscience. To hold here in Greek means to be able or possessed with. As Timothy understands God's destiny for him and the gifts that God had deposited in him, he would be abled or possessed with faith. This would nurture and keep him through until the performance, perfection and completion of the prophetic word and gifts imparted to him.

The apostle Paul tells young Timothy not to neglect the adventure God placed within him. He said, "God has exciting things planned for you! Sure, they involve risks, but take the risks, and you will arrive at your destination or destiny." In Latin, res adventura means a thing about to happen. The dictionary defines adventure as an undertaking of uncertain outcome; a hazardous enterprise; an exciting or very unusual experience; participation in exciting enterprises or undertakings; to take a chance; to take the risk involved. Advenare in Latin means to arrive.

The adventure tests our will and our skills. It summons forth talent and abilities that have been lying dormant awaiting our embarkation.

Paul encourages Timothy not to neglect his own personal adventure. Neglect in Greek, ameleo (am-el-eh-o), means to make light of; not regard; be careless of. Melo (mel-o) in Greek means to be of interest; to concern; to take care; or, it matters. The "a" placed in front of melo negates the meaning of the word; therefore, ameleo means it does not matter. Paul says to Timothy, "Son, never say that your adventure does not matter!"

When I call to remembrance the unfeigned faith
that is in thee ... and I am persuaded that in thee also.
Wherefore I put thee in remembrance that thou stir up
the gift of God, which is in thee by the putting on of
my hands (2 Timothy 1:5, 6, KJV).

Paul is speaking into the life and destiny of his spiritual son. He is admonishing him never to let his fire go out. He is telling him to stir up (anazopureo) a compound of an, "again," zoe, "life," and pur, "fire" a life fire; a fire inside. The word means to rekindle or resuscitate. It is in the present tense in Greek, which speaks of progressive, continuous action. The Greek scholar A.T. Robertson translates "stir up" as keep blazing. Paul says to Timothy, "Son, go for it! God has placed a rich treasure in you, and He has not given to you the spirit of fear or timidity. You will succeed, I absolutely know it. I believe in you. You are destined for great things. When revelation knowledge seizes this insight into destiny and adventure, no one will stop you. Gifts, talents, aptitudes and genius will surge from the depths of your being. Pursuing God and His adventure will thrill and exhilarate you!"

God has placed a fire of adventure inside us. Stir it, stoke it, prod it and provoke it. Seek the genius within you. It has been said that geniuses take domains where they have never gone before. Usually, this is because they stand on the shoulders of those who have come before them and see further. God has given gifts to you and all people. He is reconciling all things back to Himself. Every domain belongs to the Father and Creator of all things. It is the ambassadorial task of the citizens of the Kingdom of God to reconcile all things back to the original author and owner. An ambassador is a diplomatic official of the highest rank representing his government on a temporary mission. The ambassador is an authorized messenger or representative. An ambassador at large is not assigned to a particular diplomatic post, but is on a special mission. All citizens of the Kingdom of God are ambassadors at large. Jesus Christ was God the Father's Ambassador Extraordinary and Plenipotentiary inasmuch as He represented the Kingdom of Light against the kingdom of darkness.

Today God is doing a new and great thing in the earth. The kingdoms of commerce, knowledge, communication; the structures, systems, and institutions of this world must come under the rulership of the supreme Potentate of the universe, Jesus Christ. God is the One Who has deposited genius in you. It must be identified, cultivated and deployed. The genius possesses inventive capability in his or her domain. God wants to give you a breakthrough idea or insight. So sit before Him in worship. Surrender all your gifts, accomplishments, education, training, resources and processes to His Lordship. Ask Him to bless your mind in all of its splendour!

God promises to bless the works of His covenant children's hands. Works are transactions, activities, products, property, business, deeds, things or wares of your making, occupation, operations, handiwork and workmanship. Hands in the Bible imply force, power, capacity and direction. How splendid! How magnificent! Meditate upon this until it explodes into your spirit in revelation knowledge. You and I have been endowed by Almighty God with genius capacity for divinely sanctioned product development. There are supernatural business deeds and transactions awaiting the application of your God-given gifts. Even if no one discovered your domain of genius early on, it is not too late. Satan has wanted to destroy your genius, but God has redeemed your life from destruction. The supernatural person of the Holy Spirit has taken up residence in you. Things that were dead are coming back to life. Dreams, visions, abilities, genius. Do not be afraid to seek God for something great. I have prayed and asked God to make something out of me.

You and I share a passion—no, more than a passion, a raging inferno of desire for all the world to know how great and mighty our Father is! May he use us to exhibit His great power and mercy to all the billions of people on this planet. God is calling you to make no small plans, to dream no small dreams, to pray no small prayers, to harbor no small expectations. You are a potential genius. Your greatest days of passion, purpose and productivity are ahead of you. The Father wants to make you a master negotiator in the affairs of the Kingdom. How can we surrender to mediocrity when the Spirit of Almighty God resides within us?

> That you may really come to know practically,
> through experience for yourselves the love of
> Christ, which far surpasses mere knowledge
> without experience; that you may be filled through
> all your being unto all the fullness of God, may
> have all the richest measure of the Divine
> Presence and become a body wholly filled and
> flooded with God Himself! Now to Him Who, by

81

(in consequence of) the action of His power that is at work within us, is able to carry out His purpose and do superabundantly, far over and above all that we dare ask or think, infinitely beyond our highest prayers, desires, thoughts, hopes or dreams—To Him be glory in the church and in Christ Jesus throughout all generations forever and ever. Amen (so be it).
(Ephesians 3:19, 20, Amplified Bible)

The structured domains of mathematics, music, chess, ballet, drawing and so on are, of course, not the only domains in which genius may be realized. A business or civic leader who is honest, future-oriented, inspiring and competent may demonstrate genius in his or her work. Men such as George Washington, Robert E. Lee, Stonewall Jackson, Napoleon, Hannibal and Wellington all demonstrated genius in military command. Adolph Hitler was a genius, though an evil one. This brutal, evil murderer of more than six million Jews performed feats of wonder in Germany. Hitler revived a bankrupt, debt- and deficit-riddled economy. In four years, he balanced the budget and paid off the debt. He erased Germany's fifty percent unemployment rate by establishing training schools for the unskilled. He almost completely eradicated crime, he built freeways, and he promised the production of an automobile affordable by all Germans. Hitler also reclaimed the Rhineland and rejected the Treaty of Versailles. He restored national pride and purpose.Hitler is an example of how genius may be employed in the service of evil as well as good.

A great example of the latter is Bill Cosby, educator, television pioneer, actor philanthropist, comedian, cultural critic and genius. Coming from a background of poverty and tragedy, he certainly has become the senior statesman for the art and craft of comedic storytelling. Challenging stereotypes both in I-Spy and The Cosby Show, Cosby, through his dignity, intelligence, sensitivity and creativity, has created positive and powerful images of and for African American. Mr. Cosby and his wife's philanthropic commitment to the education of America's youth is historic in its breadth and depth.

Another notable example of genius is found in the late Japanese entrepreneur, philosopher and philanthropist Konosuke Matsushita (Mat-SOSH-ta). He was the last child born into a family of ten. His father had a gambling problem, and by the time little Konosuke was four years old, his father gambled away all his family's possessions. The family had to radically alter its lifestyle, moving from a twelve-room house to one with three rooms. Living in extreme poverty, Konosuke lost three of his siblings in 1901. By 1919, he was the lone survivor in his family.

Interviews conducted with Konosuke's childhood acquaintances reveal nothing special that could have predicted his eventual success. He began working for himself in 1917 with one hundred yen, no formal education or contacts, and a history of poverty and family decompensation. He did not have looks—as an adult, he was five feet, five inches tall, weighed one hundred thirty-five pounds and had protruding ears. What he did have was vision and an unquenchable fire to succeed.

His goals were noble in that he did not pursue wealth and fame, but rather the power to do good and bring about change that wealth and prestige allow. He sought to eradicate poverty and war, to raise the aspirations and education of the Japanese people, and to secure for them a place of note and dignity in the world. By 1950, Matsushita Electrical Industrial, which began with five workers, employed more than ten thousand. Now, MEI, sometimes called Japan's General Electric, generates $65 billion in annual revenue.

After the atomic bombs were dropped on Hiroshima and Nagasake on August 6 and 9, 1945, Matsushita rebuilt his companies and forged ahead with the same vision and determination that had fueled him before the war. He gave away hundreds of millions of dollars, built a graduate-level leadership training institute in Japan, and established the Japan Prize, a prize acknowledging laudable scientific accomplishment by scientists of all nationalities. The prize is worth approximately $900,000 today.

Matsushita's story inspires and inflames the soul with hope and possibility. He believed that those born or thrust into the most crippling circumstances have the power to overcome their plight and make a contribution to the betterment of the world. He believed that if we would demand more and more of ourselves, if we would see setbacks as opportunities, if we would learn from hardships and failures, that we, too, would be capable of meaningful things. In spite of great wealth and influence, Matsushita remained a humble teacher and student all his life. He was a prime example of the fire of genius.

I want you to capture the notion of how hard the so-called genius works. Matsushita was driven and hardworking. Another genius, Nikola Tesla, has been called the patron saint of modern electricity. Tesla's inventions include the induction motor, the electrical-power distribution system, fluorescent and neon lighting, wireless communication, robotics, even the remote control. Tesla biographer Marc Seifer credits Tesla with creating "the technological backbone of the modern era."

Young Nikola's fascination with flight began at age three. He was inventing things even as a boy. He created a propeller driven by either sewing or gluing sixteen May bugs four abreast on the wooden blades.

Tesla's father, Milutin, an omnivorous reader, owned a large library, so information was readily available to Nikola and his siblings. His mother, Djouka, descended from a long line of inventors. Tesla says she conceived many ingenious kitchen tools. He credits his mother for his inventive fire. As a university student, Tesla studied up to twenty hours each day. He majored in engineering and languages.

Courage, enterprise, perseverance and an insatiable curiosity all characterize the realm of genius in these people and in anyone. Genius has much to do with vision, with different ways of seeing things and with challenging the status quo. Whether Einstein, Tesla, George Washington Carver or Edison, geniuses are imagineers. Einstein biographer Ronald Clark has written that Einstein's faith in his powers of imagination gave him the courage to challenge accepted dogma in the physical sciences.

However, not all things need to be challenged. There are permanent things that do not. But many paradigms do need to be challenged, many frontiers need to be pushed back.

In the preface to his book Genius Talk, Denis Brian writes:

> Almost everything is still a mystery: the why, when and how of the universe and its inhabitants. The vagaries of human behavior and subatomic particles seem equally inscrutable. Is our world an incredible accident, or has it a purpose? What is there left to discover? Are our brains—made from the same atoms as stars—simply sophisticated computers or something more? God not being avail able, I looked for scientists on the cutting edge, the brightest and most daring thinkers of our time ...

The fact is that God is available. The late Francis A. Schaeffer said, "He is there, and He is not silent. It is time for Christians to stop shying away from so-called worldly pur-suits. Science, business and every other domain are all the legitimate province of Christianity.

We all owe it to God to maximally develop whatever gifts, talents, capacities or abilities He has given us. It's sim-ple: Mediocrity does not serve the purposes of God. There is a fire within you to change something. Commit yourself to it. This is your genius—the God-given power to change something for good. Become the benefactor of humanity. Force the people around you to realize a higher quality of life. Let them see that there are worthwhile things in which they can invest their God-given treasures. This is your genius. Inspire and infire people. Lead them out of self-pity and resignation into the great adventure. Lead them beyond themselves. Lead them to true redemption that only comes through God and His total plan and purposes.

Alexander Hamilton (1755-1804), George Washington's wartime aide-de-camp, co-framer of the U.S. Constitution, principal author of the Federalist Papers (51 of 85 issues) and Secretary of the Treasury from 1789-1795, was called by some a genius. Here is what Hamilton himself wrote about it:

> Men give me credit for genius. All the genius I have lies just on this: When I have a subject in hand, I study it profoundly. Day and night it is before me. I explore it in all its bearings. My mind becomes pervaded with it. Then the effort which I made the people are pleased to call the fruit of genius. It is the fruit of labor and thought.

Another genius, Dr. Jonas Salk, discoverer of the polio vaccine, worked sixteen to eighteen hours a day, six days a week for five years in pursuit of an effective immunization against the crippling disease of polio. Another, Leonardo Da Vinci, is universally noted as one of the world's greatest geniuses, although he had a very inauspicious start. Da Vinci came from a broken home. He never saw his mother, and while he was young, his father married a sixteen-year-old girl. For the first twelve years of young Leonardo's life, one of his grandmothers and two of his aunts raised him. After that he went to live with his father and stepmother.

Because Leonardo's father was a lawyer, he was considered better than the other children living in his village and was not allowed to play with them. So young Leonardo became a loner. Therefore, as a boy, he curiously hiked the countryside, fascinated with everything. Everything in nature arrested his curiosity. Despite his unstable background, over time, his careful observations made him an expert on dozens of artistic and scientific subjects. Da Vinci gained distinction as an astronomer, a geologist, an engineer, a botanist, an anatomist, an author, an illustrator and a psychologist. He also became a famous painter. Leonardo Da Vinci worked hard to cultivate his genius.

Da Vinci was not unlike many people recognized as geniuses today, who had ordinary or unusually difficult beginnings. For instance, Napoleon stood forty-second in his military academy class. Booker T. Washington was born a slave and had a difficult early life. He went on to distinguish himself as one of the leading educators of his time. Great scientist Michael Faraday began at the anvil of a blacksmith. Shakespeare was a horse valet at one of London's theaters before he became a towering literary figure. Astronomer Copernicus began in a barber shop. Christopher Columbus was the son of a weaver. Homer, the great Greek author of

The Iliad and Odyssey, was the son of a small farmer. Abraham Lincoln was a rail-splitter.

The list goes on. Homer and John Milton, author of Paradise Lost and Paradise Regained, were both blind. Beethoven was deaf. Thomas Edison lost almost all his hearing at age twelve. Alexander the Great was hunchbacked. Miguel Cervantes, author of Don Quixote, overcame stuttering to become a powerful public speaker. Franklin Roosevelt, a cripple and the thirty-second and longest-serving president (Democrat, 1933-1945), has been called by some America's greatest president. Winston Churchill, no less a giant, called Roosevelt "the greatest American we have ever known and the greatest champion of freedom who has ever brought aid and comfort from the New World to the Old."

These men prove that genius in any area is less the fruit of genetics than of vision, hard work, determination, focus, perseverance and gratitude. Yes, gratitude. Gratitude for the gifts of curiosity, sustained concentration and discovery. Gratitude to God, the Giver of all good and perfect gifts.

Seventeenth-Century composer George Frideric Handel was and is considered a genius. But he, too, had a rough beginning. Handel is most famous for his work "Messiah." It has been written that this work "has probably done more to convince thousands of mankind that there is a God about us than all the theological works ever written." Handel was a man of God, a man of prayer and a man of musical genius.

In 1741, having experienced failure after failure, in poor health and on the verge of being thrown into debtors' prison, Handel shut himself in the house on August 22 and began to compose. Twenty-four days later, all 260 pages of the manuscript were completed. For three and a half weeks, Handel did not leave his house. When he emerged, he gave the world a great gift of music that has continued to stand the test of time. In spite of pressures and stresses, this man of God, this genius of God, brought forth a gift to the world.

Handel had seen men all around him with less talent being honored and acclaimed by society. He wrestled with depression, disillusion and exasperation. But he refused to give up. He had to produce music. He owed it to God to cultivate the genius God had placed inside him.

So do you and I owe it to God to cultivate the gift He has placed inside us. It is unacceptable to think lightly of God's gifts. The world needs your genius, the fire burning inside you. You will never know peace or contentment until you answer the call of God. The moment you say yes to the call and gift of God in your life, you will begin to experience the peace of having embarked on your life's journey. There are tens, thousands, maybe even millions of people waiting for you to preach, to paint, to compose, to design, to lead, to pioneer, to innovate, to write, to build, to produce, to manufacture.

Our generation owes a great debt to history. We have inherited a legacy of genius, a legacy of leadership and sacrifice. We cannot leave the succeeding generation spiritually, culturally, intellectually, artistically, morally, politically or institutionally bankrupt The Sovereign God of history is placing great demands upon this generation. Passive religion and other worldly spirituality will leave the succeeding generation with no roadmaps.

We must spend ourselves in the service of God and humanity. This means each of us being called upon by God in this hour must work with vigor. The world is in need of lamplighters, of torchbearers, of standard-raisers. Arise, awake from slumber! Allow God to stir you to the very depths of your being. Allow Him to wrest from you the absolute all and best you can give. Go forth in obedience, raise the standard, and someone, somewhere, someday may call you God's genius.

The Fire Inside

5

THE WORLD OF THE CHILD

It was and is the will of Almighty God that all children be born in joy and unto great purpose and destiny. However, because of the sin of the first human parents, this is generally not the case.

After the disobedience of Eve and Adam in the Garden of Eden, God had to modify the dominion mandate found in Genesis 1:26-28. God does not revoke the command for the first humans to be fruitful and multiply, but He says to the woman:

> ...I will greatly multiply thy sorrow and thy conception; in sorrow thou shalt bring forth children ... (Genesis 3:16, KJV).

"Sorrow" here is the Hebrew word meaning worry, pain, anger, displeasure, grief, hurt, to make sorry, vexation, worship. "Children" is from the Hebrew word meaning son or builder of the family name; subject, nation, quality or condition; anointed or appointed one; mighty man, soldier, son, valiant whelp, worthy young one. This verse reveals not only that pain is to be involved in the bringing forth of individual children, but even the birth of nations will be a thing of vexation or worship. Isn't this true? Nations historically have been either a source of vexation or an object of worship. God never sees anything insignificant in the womb. That is why this particular pronouncement was so devastating.

The original intent of God was that every child born would be the recipient of love, security, nurture and destiny. With this pronouncement, a mother became just as likely to loathe a child she had carried in her womb for nine months. This is against the divine plan of God.

God's original plan was to populate the earth with humans that would obey Him, and in so doing, command the earth under the Dominion Mandate to bring forth of its good treasures. God wanted man to enjoy the earth. God wanted man to enjoy fellowship with Him. God wanted man to discover the outer reaches of his potential within the framework of the laws that govern creation. I believe each generation was to successively contribute to the growing canon of revelation knowledge and experience. Each generation would be entrusted with generating something specific. This is still the case. God has expectations of each succeeding generation. So when satan, who hates all children, particularly the seed of the godly, attacks children, he is ultimately attacking God and His eternal purposes. Redemption breaks the curse of Genesis 3:16 and restores our understanding of the purposes of childbearing.

We understand the proliferation of out-of-wedlock births plays into the hands of satan. Notice that in God's original of things, He created parents, not children. So there was family consisting of God, then human father and mother.

This is still divine order for the day. God, a relationship between Him and the human father and mother, the union between the two humans, then the bringing forth of children. God also had set Adam and Eve in His place of provision. In God's mind Eden, along with His spoken word, were to create the aspirations for the first humans. However, Adam and Eve found the tree of the knowledge of good and evil too irresistible for their own good. They ate against God's instructions, sin entered, death entered by sin, and the world has never been the same

God never intended for children to be encumbered by sin and death. God planned for the first children to live in the Garden of Eden's lap of luxury. He intended for them to frolic by the four rivers and sample the delicious fruit growing on Eden's permissible trees. The sparkling diamonds, emeralds and sapphires littering the ground would excite the children in play. The first children would get to see God face to face and hear His voice. They would recognize Him, for their dad, Adam, possessed some of His characteristics. They would never know poverty, disease, pain, hunger, homelessness, war, Godlessness, divorce, mental or emotional disease, or death. However, before God could fulfill His desire to bless the first children, the first parents sinned, plunging the whole earth into convulsions and dooming their first offspring to life in broken communion with God outside the garden.

Instead of telling his children about the great things God had done for them, His great mercy and generosity, Adam had to tell them that he had broken covenant with God, lost their home and forfeited their eternal privileges. He had to tell them, "You were not supposed to know separation from God, disease or death, but because of me, you will.
I squandered away your eternal inheritance. Your mother obeyed the voice of satan, and I followed her, though we had a clear word from God. So we've cursed you."

Instead, Adam was supposed to have been able to tell his children, "Obey God as I have done, and surely He will bless you all the days of your eternal lives." They were supposed to have learned obedience from their parents. But they were given a legacy of disobedience and judgment.

Now every child born on the planet inherits not the nature of God through obedient first Adam, but the nature of that first Adam who rebelled against God. Secular man hates the notion that he is a sinner. He believes himself to be his own God. This is folly of extreme magnitude. But even this reveals man's quest to return to the image he possessed before man's fall. God desires man to be in His image. Man wants the image of God on his own terms, but this is not possible. The restoration of the image of God in man only comes through the voluntary acceptance of the restorative and regenerative work of Jesus Christ at the cross. Although secular humanist man despises the lowliness of the cross, the cross is his only help. It is the quintessential, unsurpassed display of Almighty God's love for sinful man.

In fact, Jesus Christ is called the Last Adam in the Bible because He came to restore, through His own obedience humanity that had been separated from God through the first Adam's disobedience. Every child born onto this planet is born with the nature of the first Adam to parents who have either the nature of the first or Second Adam. This is the child's first experience of his or her own little world.

Whether a child comes into a first environment of redemption or irredemption, it is the will of God that every human being on earth succeed in his or her divine calling and purpose. God created the ultimate success environment in the beginning; it was called the Garden of Eden. Eden means paradise. It was a place of inexplicable beauty, yet with boundaries. Even paradise has laws. Man was created by God to be a creature of laws. Laws are intended to preserve man's communion with God and to make possible his productivity. Communion with God in the place of His appointment, under the authority of His law, is the most productive place in the universe.

The first Adam was to teach his offspring or seed to hear the voice of God. The first Adam's children were to be taught by their parents to expand the model of paradise over the entire creation, bringing the whole of the physical under the rule of God through spiritual law. All the nations destined to inhabit earth were in the loins of the first Adam. Again, this is why childbirth is so important to God. The fate of nations is in the loins of men. Through the disobedience of the first Adam, every nation to inhabit the earth is born with the nature of sin, of disobedience toward God.

God is passionate about blessing the whole of humanity. We know this because when Adam forfeited man's righteous inheritance, God immediately instituted a plan to get it
back. Man's covenant of obedience or disobedience to God
has enormous historical and national consequences. Right
now, every man and woman on earth is carrying not only the
future and destiny of their own seed, but that of the nation to
which God has called them.

In Genesis 6-9, God sought to preserve a godly seed of
the human race through Noah. Every human being on earth
died, except Noah and his family. Noah was spared because
God saw he was a righteous man. You can imagine how awesome a responsibility it is to be the first man to carry out the
purposes of God in filling the earth with godly seed. Now the
mantle falls upon you.

Behold the love and patience of our Father: Adam
fails, but God is so committed to His purpose that He starts
all over again with the Noah family.

> And God blessed Noah and his sons, and said unto
> them, Be fruitful, and multiply, and replenish the
> earth. And you, be ye fruitful, and multiply;
> bring forth abundantly in the earth, and multiply
> therein (Genesis 9:1, 7, KJV).

Genesis 11 states that all the nations of the earth came
out of the loins of Noah and his three sons. This is awesome.
All the seed of the first Adam are dead except Noah, Shem,
Ham, Japheth and their wives. They were under the covering
of Noah's obedience.

In Genesis, we see that the power, passion and purpose for the building of cities and the development of culture and technology are resident in the spirit of man. This is the gift of God and should be used to worship and glorify Him.

The Noahic experiment lasted until Genesis chapter II when man used his technological skills and the unity of the Noahic line to build a monument to itself. God does not have a problem with great accomplishment; it is He Who has placed within us the ability to achieve great things. However, everything man achieves must be attributed to the goodness, mercy and kindness of the Almighty Creator who has endowed man with all his capacities.

So in Genesis 11, God has to destroy the Tower of Babel. Genesis 11:3 (KJV) says:

> And they said one to another, Go to, let us make brick, and burn them thoroughly. And they had brick for stone, and slime had they for mortar.

The Tower of Babel was constructed by that which man had made. You will notice that the Temple of Moses and the Tabernacle of David both were constructed of cut stones, that which God had made. In a sense, the Tower of Babel is a rejection of the Creator. The Babylonian Creation Epic says the people molded bricks for a whole year. The literal name for the structure called the Tower of Babel is E-sag-ila, or the house whose head is lifted up. The uppermost part of the structure was called E-temen-an-ki, or house of the foundation of heaven and earth. A Babylonian document dating in the Third Century B.C. says the tower was seven stories high.

In biblical numerology, the number seven represents spiritual perfection. Six in the Bible is the number of man, plus one being seven. The Hebrew word for seven is shevah, from the root savah, meaning to be full or satisfied; to have enough of. Another word, sahvath, means to cease, desist or rest; and the word Shabbath, Sabbath, or day of rest. Shagavh means to swear or make an oath. Hence, the number seven points to the idea of the satisfaction or fullness of an oath. In fact, the same word for seven is used for oath. The word deals with the security, satisfaction, fullness of the obligation, and completeness of the bond of an oath or covenant.

Genesis 1:1 consists of seven words and twenty-eight letters, thus seven connotes revelation. This is significant because Genesis is the most important statement made in the Bible, or anywhere else in all of literature, secular or so-called divine. God establishes the basis for all interaction with Him and the creation in Genesis 1:1.

So the building of the Tower of Babel was not merely a technological feat. In the building of this structure, man was making a statement of philosophy and of religion. He was declaring himself to be his own god. He was declaring himself independent of God as the Creator and Revelator. He was declaring himself an independent knower, as Eve and Adam had done in the garden. By building this tower, man was declaring war against God. He was placing his ability to "know" through the application of the rational processes of his own mind superior to knowing through God's revelation of His Creation. He was declaring his right to determine who he would worship and how.

In building the tower, man was attempting to recreate creation and to devise his own Sabbath, his own rest. This is where comparative religion and the New Age movement were re-born; they had been born in the Garden of Eden. It is the work of satan and the powers of darkness. The Tower of Babel caused spiritual confusion and blindness to be foisted upon humanity.

The Tower of Babel and the city of Babylon represent the city of man in the Bible. That is, the city of man in opposition to the city of God. Eden and Babylon represent rival kingdoms with rival plans. Babylon and the tower were beautiful for the eyes to behold. The city of Babylon and its gardens made up one of the seven wonders of the world. However, they were not beautiful to God. He destroyed the tower, and all that the spiritual city of Babylon represents is cursed by God. The salvation of God comes to deliver us from the effects of spiritual Babylon. All that is darkness (ignorance, spiritual death), arrogance, exaltation of man, worship of the creation and creature more than the Creator, and the resultant social, institutional, cultural and national death, is the fruit of spiritual Babylon. The edifice of ungodly philosophies, lofty reasoning and dark illogic that conspire to deny God make up the fruit of the Tower.

God never intended the world of the child to be a dark world. God's light and love permeated the Garden of Eden. God's wisdom and knowledge were available to man. The Church is rightfully concerned about the moral legacy one generation leaves to another.

We should be just as concerned about the intellectual legacy. Men aspire, build, govern, earn, bequeath, socialize, commune and entertain themselves on the basis of their intellectual and spiritual presuppositions, their worldview. One generation is responsible to the next in every way. If we leave the succeeding generation darkness, ignorance, apathy, cynicism, despair, debt, ungodliness, unrighteousness, humanism, evolutionism, greed, political non-astuteness, lack of a realization of national purpose, the death of common sense, crumbling institutional foundations and garbled social discourse, we curse the nation to mediocrity and condemnation.

This world, the world of the children, needs heroes. Turbulent, cynical times cry out for heroic living. Every child comes to this planet with a special destiny. Yet since 1973, satan has denied many of them by murdering more than 150 million children through abortion. Perhaps among them was a Moses, a Joshua, a Gideon, a Miriam, a Deborah or an Esther. Life equals destiny, so when satan murders a child, he is assaulting the purposes of God on earth. When satan murders a child, he is attacking history and the destiny, the future of nations. Each unborn generation carries in it the future of a nation. That future is determined largely by the legacy left by the generation carrying the future generation in its loins.

Think about it. The first family was intended by God to be the ultimate breeding ground for success. Free from spiritual or economic constraints, in an atmosphere of love, grounded in spiritual law, Adam and Eve were to be free to cultivate their seed. Instead they were born into a generational curse. The first Adam doomed his seed to distraction and confusion of purpose.

However, salvation restores the family as the breeding ground for success. God teaches us in the Bible that every child has a purpose. This is found in Proverbs 22:6:

Train up a child in the way he should go and in
keeping with his individual gift or bent, and
when he is old he will not depart from it (Amplified
Bible).

In Roget's Thesaurus, the word "bent" has these syn-onyms: talent, flair, gift, endowment, genius, instinct, faculty, power, ability, capability, capacity, potential, caliber, aptitude, propensity, gift for, genius for and so on.

"Train" is the Hebrew word chanak (khaw-nak). It means to initiate or discipline; to narrow the focus. Chanak is from a root meaning to consecrate or dedicate. The word for child in Proverbs 22:6 literally means a boy or girl from the age of infancy to adolescence. It is the word na'ar. Interestingly, na'ar also means wandering one, or one tossed about.

"Way" is the Hebrew word derek (deh-rek), meaning a road; a course of life or a course of action; a journey, a custom; to string a bow; to guide, or lead forth.

"Go" means portion, appointment, commandment, to eat, have entry; mind, mouth, part, portion; sound speech, two-edged sword; to blow away; scatter to the four corners.

Therefore, when God blesses us with children, He is allowing us to shape the future. The way we train our children determines history. When God gives us children, He is entrusting us with His purposes.

But the Word says children are prone to wandering. That is why we, as parents, must identify their potential and latent genius, then narrow their focus, so as to prepare them for that which God has appointed as their portion. Their portion will involve their minds in preparation and their mouths for provision. Your child has sound speech and a two-edged sword for a specific area in the creation of God. It was planned from before the foundation of the world that our children would have an appointment from God that would cause their sound speech to be scattered to the four winds, to the four corners of the earth.

According to the Hebrew language, when you are training your child in his or her destiny, you are stringing a bow. God uses the bow to attack and destroy wickedness.

> He shall flee from the iron weapon, and the bow
> of steel shall strike him through (Job 20:24, KJV).
> As arrows are in the hand of a mighty man; so are
> children of the youth (Psalm 127:4, KJV).

"Arrow" means a piercer; a wound; a thunderbolt; to cut, split or divide.

God gives us children as bows and arrows against the forces of darkness in their generations. Our children, our seed will divide the kingdom of darkness. They will pierce and wound satan and his demons in their generations. They will go in to battle a skilled force of steel warriors for the Lord and His righteous Kingdom. They will be a mighty prophetic army, unlike any seen in a long time. They are being trained on the anvil of purpose.

> Lo, children are an heritage of the Lord: and the
> fruit of the womb is His reward (Psalm 127:3, KJV).

"Heritage" means occupancy; to cause to, make to possess. Children are a possession of the Lord, and I believe a generation is coming that will act the part, that will not be destroyed through drugs, alcohol, promiscuous sex, rejection, fear, perversion or devil worship. God is raising Josephs and Daniels in all nations. But they need special mentoring and cultivation. They need special refinement and impartation. Their anointings must be protected. They are among a generation that, even in their youth, need to see their parents trust the Lord for mighty deeds and exploits. Our children are pushing us to excel in the Lord and to leave them a legacy of faith. Faith tried and purified. The embryo of their destiny is summoning forth from our generation a greater accountability to the purposes of God. Let us respond to the call.

When they see us excel in the Lord, they too will want to be obedient to His covenant. And God is guaranteeing the success of your children in return for their obedience, as proved in Psalm 112:1-8 .

> Praise ye the Lord. Blessed is the man that feareth
> the Lord, that delighteth greatly in his command-

ments. His seed shall be mighty upon earth: the generation of the upright shall be blessed. Wealth and riches shall be in his house: and his righteousness endureth for ever. Unto the upright there ariseth light in the darkness: he is gracious, and full of compassion, and righteous. A good man sheweth favour, and lendeth: he will guide his affairs with discretion. Surely he shall not be moved for ever: the righteous shall be in everlasting remembrance. He shall not be afraid of evil tidings: his heart is fixed, trusting in the Lord. His heart is established, he shall not be afraid, until he see his desire upon his enemies (KJV).

When you enter into covenant with the Almighty God, He promises to bless your seed. He told Abraham that his seed would be as the sand on the beach and the stars in the sky. This promise was made to a man whose wife was barren at the time. God also promised Abraham that his seed would possess the gate of their enemies, and that they would bless the entire earth. Psalm 25:12, 13 states:

What man is he that feareth the Lord? him shall he teach in the way that he shall choose. His soul shall dwell at ease; and his seed shall inherit the earth (KJV).

Another of these covenant promises is found in Psalm 37:25, 26:

I have been young, and now am old; yet have I not seen the righteous forsaken, nor his seed begging

bread. He is ever merciful, and lendeth; and his seed is
blessed (KJV).

Yet another example:
The children of thy servants shall continue, and
their seed shall be established before thee. (Psalm
102:28, KJV).

The promise also is found in Deuteronomy:

Now these are the commandments, the statutes, and
the judgments, which the Lord your God commanded
to teach you, that ye might do them in the land
whither ye go to possess it: That thou mightest
fear the Lord thy God, to keep all his statutes
and his commandments, which I command thee,
thou, and thy son, and thy son's son, all the days of thy
life; and that thy days may be prolonged. Hear
therefore, O Israel, and observe to do it; that
it may be well with thee, and that ye may increase
mightily, as the Lord God of thy fathers hath promised thee, in the land that floweth with milk and
honey.

Hear, O Israel: The Lord our God is one Lord: And
thou shalt love the Lord thy God with all thine
heart, and with all thy soul, and with all thy
might. And these words, which I command thee this
day, shall be in thine heart: And thou shalt teach them
diligently unto thy children, and shalt talk of them
when thou sittest in thine house, and when thou
walkest by the way, and when thou lyest down, and

when thou risest up (Deuteronomy 6:1-7, KJV).

The Bible is full of these covenant promises concerning the blessing of God upon our seed in return for covenantal obedience. This is awesome because their blessing is not dependent upon anything other than the covenantal faithfulness of God to His Word, and their own obedience to His righteous requirements.

What a tremendous blessing it is to be able to speak guaranteed success into the life and future of your child. Each night when I pray with my sons, I thank God for the great destiny to which He has called them, and for its fulfillment. I tell them that if they only obey God and serve Him, their lives will be the most incredible adventure. If they obey God, they will meet people, go places and have experiences they otherwise would never have had. I talk to them about teaching their own seed to obey and serve God and to trust Him for great things.

The world of the child should be permeated with the Word of God. Children should be exposed to the prophetic voice early in their lives. In Genesis 49, the patriarch Jacob (Israel) prophesied destiny over his grandchildren. Destiny does not begin in adulthood. Destiny is the seed contained in a person at birth. In fact, in Jeremiah chapter one and Isaiah chapter forty-nine, both of these prophets acknowledged that they were called from their mothers' wombs. The child should have prophetic destiny confirmed over their lives as early as possible. Jesus flowed under a heavy and constant anointing with the approval and affirmation of the Father.

We must be cautious regarding who we allow to speak into the lives of our children. The human spirit is very sensitive to words, and the wrong ones can be devastating. That is why often a word of death spoken over our lives in childhood follows us into our adult years. This word of death may have killed your faith in an area. This word of death must be uprooted by the Word of Life, which is the Word of God.

We should allow those who know the Counsel of the Father, and who have the Word of the Lord in their mouths to speak into the worlds of our children. Both the written and the spoken word create faith. Every time we speak, we are causing either life or death to come forth (Proverbs 18:21). The spoken word through the mouth of a prophet of God has altered the course of individuals and nations. Read the God's Word translation of 1 Corinthians 14:3 concerning prophecy:

> But when a person speaks what God has revealed, he speaks to people to help them grow, to encourage them, and to comfort them.
>
> But on the other hand, the one who prophesies, who interprets the divine will and purpose ... speaks to men for their up building and constructive spiritual progress and encouragement and consolation (Amplified).

One Greek scholar translates "prophesies" in 1 Corinthians 14:3 as imparting of divine revelations to men. Prophecy confirms destiny and waters the seeds of greatness and positive expectancy. God has given you genius potential and called your child to a great destiny. Begin to speak the

Word of faith over your child today, now. If you do not know what God has called your child to, ask Him. Study the child. What sorts of things interest him or her? Be careful not to impose upon him or her your own unfulfilled dreams. Those are for you, not your child. Do not defer your destiny and saddle your child with the fruit of your own disobedience and unbelief.

Words create (Genesis 1; Romans 4:17). When you have a revelation of your child's destiny, begin to speak it over him or her every day. Expose your child to it. Let him or her touch it, feel it, think it, imagine it. If someone you know is doing what your child is called to do, take your child there. Expose him or her to the sights, sound, knowledge and nuances of whatever it is. Use your child's destiny both to positively instruct and to discipline. Lay your hands upon him or her and decree the fulfillment of God's purpose.

Children are fascinated by everything. Do not kill their curiosity in the name of religion. Children are creatures of wonder, amazement and faith. They love to draw, paint, sing, make up games and play with make-believe friends. Children are creative by nature and often want to improve on our ways of doing and seeing things. This is not always a bad thing. They are driven by their creative nature and the hunger of their burgeoning little spirits toward growth and mastery. Children have creative expectations. Just watch them become frustrated over the drawing that did not come out the way they wanted. This is a wonderful opportunity to teach them that it is okay to have high expectations, but that the higher the expectation, the more patience is demanded to nurture the project through to completion.

Impart to your child the joy and love of learning. He or she may rebel in the short term against reading and writing reports, but the long-term payoff is well worth it. Seeds of greatness are planted through reading of the lives of great men and women. They are watered through reading of great historic deeds and exploits. Read the Bible together. Also read history. Tales of love and war. Tales of the rise and fall of empires. Tales of war and peace. Tales of disease and healing, of challenge and triumph. Teach them the history of your nation and its purpose. Teach children of their own holy men, prophets and sages. Teach them of great scientists and inventors, of so-called robber barons and entrepreneurs. Tell them of adventurers and pioneers. Tell them of hardships overcome and of fortunes won and lost. Tell them of the noble and the savage. Tell them of Genghis and Attila, of Cromwell and Luther. Tell them of slave ships and great empires. Tell them of the abolitionist movements. Rehearse history in their ears, the good and the bad, the sublime and the ridiculous. Give them lofty aspirations, and Godly confidence to go forth in preparation for a meaningful life.

But we must teach our children to be humble and gracious all the days of their lives. No matter what they may achieve, we must teach them always to give the glory to Almighty God and to treat all their fellow men with grace and dignity. We must teach them to share their bounty and good fortune and always to raise the aspirations of those around them. Teach them to be willing to fight for what is right; to spend themselves in the service of mankind. Teach them to efficiently manufacture the most excellent product and to offer it at a fair price, earning a responsible profit.

Teach them to treat their employees well, offering them incentives to outdo themselves. Challenge them through precept and example to leave the world a better place than they found it.

We must strive to leave the succeeding generation stable foundations, predictable norms, order, law, justice, fairness, a sense of the noble and the lofty, duty, honor, work, worship, saneness and common sense. We owe them a reasonably ordered world—not a world in which each man has only his own truth; where there are no ethical norms or universal standards of conduct. Not a world in which men place rights above responsibilities, and where the covenant of marriage is shunned in favor of commitment-less sex. A world where Johnny has two daddies and Sarah has two mommies. We cannot leave them a world where there is no wrong or right, good or evil, best or worst, beautiful or ugly.

We cannot leave the succeeding generation a world of positivistic philosophies where all that exists is matter. Where the human person is nothing more than a collection of atoms, where neither man nor matter are viewed as purposeful, and where the universe has no explanation. We cannot leave them so-called education that purports to train their intellects while neglecting their character in a world where they will be called upon to make enormous ethical decisions.

Instead we must teach them the power of positive decision-making, and the power of having a written mission statement. We must leave them a world of economic opportunity through free enterprise and compassionate capitalism:

not a world where hard work, vision, discipline and sacrifice are looked upon as the undesirable character traits of the greedy and aggressive. We must leave them a world where they will be judged by the content of their character and the strength of their contribution, not by their skin color or gender. We must leave them a world in which the honest pursuit of business and profit are ennobled, and where virtue and integrity are respected. A world where God is enthroned, and where America, in particular, acknowledges its incalculable debt to the Bible, and to the prayers and sacrifices of holy men and women. This is the world we must leave our children.

6

THE FIRE OF CREATIVITY

One late summer evening, my wife, Shelley, and I piled our sons into the car in response to a request that we take them out for dinner. It was a balmy Northwest evening, and the sun had just begun to set. The sky was tinged with purples and oranges, and the clouds hung lazily over the Cascade Mountains. I noticed the various species of trees and glanced out across the Puget Sound. I could not help but be taken by all the natural beauty. It struck me how varied God had been in all His creative acts. The many colors and fragrances of flowers. The different trees and plants. The oceans, rivers, streams, mountains, canyons and valleys. The splendid animal kingdom, from parrots with brilliant red, green and blue plumage to the regal lion to the busy beaver to the dignified eagle.

God also created plains, vistas, radiant stars, juicy peaches, lush green grass, not to mention all marine life, from the curious and lazy manatee to the majestic Orca whale. In fact, in the Midrash, God is called Ha-Tzayar, the Divine

Artist. He is called the Divine Architect Who uses the Torah (law) as His blueprint.

And since man is made in the image of God, he possesses an insatiable urge to create. Man as builder, designer, discoverer, tinkerer and creative creature is reflecting the image of God.

While God is the primary Creator, creating everything from nothing, man is in a secondary sense creative. Man as musician is secondarily creative inasmuch as he rearranges notes representing sounds he himself did not create. Man as painter uses primary colors he did not create. Man as sculptor fashions images out of rock that antedates his existence. Whatever the creation, when man creates, he is imitating God. It has been said, however, that man's creative impulse is only a shadow of the supernal creativity of Almighty God.

His creation was so indescribably beautiful and awe-inspiring in its pristine state that Adam questioned God about the manner in which it came to be. God said to Adam: "I created it all in six days. I created it all for you and your offspring. Now I will instruct you in what you need to know to fulfill my mandate to you on this earth." Though all of God's creation was resplendent in beauty, He chose a special place where He would commune with and instruct man. That place was the Garden of Eden. Eden, meaning paradise, or an enclosed place, was the place where Adam was to commune with and worship God. It was the place where the Rivers of Life and the Tree of Life flourished. This paradise was blessed with the Lord's abundance. It was the prototypical environment in which God desired that man live. Eden was a well-watered garden wherein were all manner of precious stones, the first sanctuary designed by God according to the pattern of heaven.

God places man in the garden to tend and cultivate it. This is man's dominion assignment. When God told Adam to keep the garden, He was telling him to protect or guard it. Robert B. Coote and David Robert Ord in The Bible's First History suggest that Eden, which means paradise, but also fenced-off place, was civilized inside, but chaos and disorder threatened outside. Coote and Ord write of the garden: "The garden is like a meticulously pruned baroque French garden. It is an oasis of order, epitomizing and projecting the royal order which exists in a world of threat."

The Garden of Eden was God's earthly sanctuary. It is the place of His government on earth. It is a type of the Church. It was to be the prototype for man's living conditions on the earth; a voluptuous paradise fenced off by the law of God.

The Garden of Eden is the School of Dominion. This is where God would instruct man in all the laws of dominion. Adam's task was to obey God in the garden, and then take the conditions of the Edenic paradise all over the world. To this end, God endowed man with the capacity for creativity, invention, art, science and so on. Man is to build godly culture all over the world.

W. Gunther Plaut in his commentary on the Torah says man's intellectual capacity bears the imprint of the Creator. He notes that though man's nature is radically different from God's (the Creator/creature distinction), man is capable of approaching God's actions. In other Jewish writings, no other man was to be like Adam in exactitude. Each man was to be created with unique qualities, which it was his own duty to perfect in the service of God and man. Failure to heed the call to perfect these qualities was believed to delay the coming of the Messiah (Acts 3:21).

Plaut notes that while the Lord did refer to His creation as very good, He never referred to it as perfect (Genesis 1:31). This is because man is to assist God in the perfecting of His creation. Man is given a holy task of work in the garden. The ancients did not see God as an abstraction; rather, He was Father, Friend and King. He also was seen as the Creative Force behind the existence of all things. God was thought to have vested all creation with purpose, and it was believed that for man to understand God was to understand his own purpose. This purpose reflects God's image. As the Bible says, man is made in the image of God (Genesis 1:26, 27). Image, the word tzelem, is related to an Akkadian word, salmu, which means statue. The word applies to Adam as a divine statue in the guise of a human. Adam was created to live a holy and righteous life under God. Adam was to be God's image in the earth.

All the beasts of the field, the fowl of the air and the fish of the sea God called upon Adam to name (Genesis 2:19, 20). Each and every living thing was brought before Adam to get named. The word "call" in Hebrew means to address, mention, address by name, pronounce or publish. To name in Genesis 2:19 is the word shem (shame), meaning to appoint, determine, charge or commit. It also means to assign definite and conspicuous position; to ordain place and purpose. Adam spoke the place and purpose of all living things over them, and God concurred. Adam passed his first dominion task with flying colors. This was also his first creative task. Creativity under the Lordship of Jesus Christ is a tool of dominion.

To remain in fellowship with God and to continue learning the task of dominion in the garden sanctuary, Adam was told not to eat of the tree in the midst of the garden (Genesis 2:16, 17). It was called the tree of the knowledge of good and evil. (Some scholars have suggested that eventually God would have instructed Adam and Eve in that particular knowledge in His own time.)

Adam and Eve failed this dominion task. In Genesis 3:6, Eve concluded that the tree was good to eat for food and to be desired to make one wise. To eat here means to consume or devour. It also means to accuse. The Bible says that Eve "saw" things about the tree. "Saw" is the word ra 'ah (raw-aw), which means to advise oneself, to consider, discern, gaze, take heed, have experience, perceive, present, provide, regard, spy, stare or think, have visions. The first seven times this word is used in Scripture it refers only to God. The eighth time, it refers to Eve.

God Himself had already said that every tree growing out of the ground was pleasant to the sight and good for food

(Genesis 2:9). The outer appearance of the tree was not the point. Eve "saw" or accused the tree of being what God already had said it was, pleasant to look at and good for food. He did not say it would make them wise. Instead, wisdom comes from the fear of the Lord and from obeying His commandments and statutes (Proverbs 1:7; 9:10; 1 Chronicles 22:12, 13). Eve began to think on her own, independently of God. She said, "What's the big deal? I think the tree will really make one wise. I think it's okay to eat some of this fruit. The serpent said I won't die, and he's probably right. I think I will become a god. I will eat of this tree." She did not use her creativity to act in God's image and perfect His creation.

Instead Eve exalted her reasoning above God's revelation. She exalted her reasoning above God's law. "Desired" means to covet or lust in Hebrew. "Make" means to do or make in the broadest sense; to accomplish, bring forth, advance, appoint, execute, furnish or fashion. "Wise" is circumspect; intelligent, expert, instruct, prosper, deal prudently, have good success, teach, to have understanding, behave oneself wisely or wittingly. God had given man the power of reason to assist with the task of dominion. But Eve allowed her reason to be aided by satan. Contrary to German philosopher Immanuel Kant and the humanists, there is no such thing as unaided reason. Man's reason is either aided by God or by satan. In fact, "one" in Genesis 3:6 means to unify; to collect one's thoughts; to go one way or another; united, alike, together.

Though God had created Adam and Eve, He had not created less-than-wise, un-Godlike creatures, and He had not told them the truth about life and death. So instead of trusting, obeying and worshipping God, Eve distrusted Him. What is worse is that she trusted herself and satan more than she did God. Eve handed Adam the fruit of the forbidden tree, and he ate it. Man became a choosing creature. The Torah teaches that yielding to Satan's temptation and eating of the fruit were two parts of the same act. Eating from the forbidden tree provided man with a moral discrimination and thereby made him capable of committing sin. By choosing to eat of this tree, Adam and Eve at once experienced the covenantal death that satan told them they would not experience. By choosing to eat of this tree, they chose sin over righteousness, expulsion from the garden, and mortality over immortality. Adam and Eve were expulsed from the garden before they could ever eat of the wonderful Tree of Life. Adam and Eve were then fallen king-priest-prophets on God's earth.

We must strive to not make the mistake Eve made and let satan interfere with our God-given ability to perfect His creation through our creativity.

The urge toward creativity was given to man by God. It is a reflection of the image of God in man. And remember, creativity under the Lordship of Jesus Christ is a tool of dominion. The urge to create is so strong in man that even the fall did not eradicate it. Fallen descendants of Adam carried on the task of dominion. In Genesis 1:26, God assigned to man the task of dominion. Dominion is from a Hebrew word meaning to subjugate, tread down, prevail against, reign, bear rule, make to rule over. Man was given the assignment of progressively bringing the entire creation under his authority as God's vice - regent, an officer appointed by a sovereign or supreme chief as his deputy.

The fallen family's first child, named Cain, worked to do just that. Cain's name means possession, acquisition, to get or acquire. His name is taken from Qanah. The root of Qanah means capital usually translated as cattle or livestock. Cain's name suggests that he initiated the history of acquisition. Cain's name also means smith or metalworker. Those of the loins of Cain were skilled in the working of metals. Genesis 4:17 acknowledges Cain as a city-builder. Abel, whose name means heir, became a shepherd, or a professor of animal husbandry.

Cain named the city he built after his son Enoch. Enoch means to consecrate the founding of. It is from the root hanakh, meaning to dedicate, train up or catechize. This root gives us the word Hanukkah. Hanukkah is the feast of the rededication of the Temple after the removal of the abomination of desecration under the Maccabees. The city of Enoch consisted of the palace, housing the royal bureaucracy and the military; the temple, representing the economic system and its religious legitimization; and the prime grain storage facility. All this was consecrated, dedicated or sacralized. Therefore, the name Enoch suggests a sacral or sacred legitimacy for the institution of the city. This is the city of man, not the city of God.

It's not that it was evil or even wrong for man to build cities. Rather, it is wrong for man to attempt to build anything that seeks to leave God out. The task of city-building was a task for dominion-minded man to carry out all over the earth, spreading Edenic conditions. City-building involves creativity; so do the tasks of tilling the ground and shepherding the sheep.

Lamech's family was also an example of fallen man pursuing dominion and the development of culture in the Bible. Lamech is the seed of the seventh generation from Adam. His name means king. Lamech and his wives Adah and Silla give birth to Yabal, Yubal, and Tubal-cain (Genesis 4:20-22). All these names are built on forms of Yabal, which means to produce. It is interesting that Cain's name of Qanah means to acquire capital, and Yabal means to produce. Yabal (Jabal) is the father of all that dwell in tents and raise cattle. Yubal (Jubal) is the father of all that handle the harp and the organ. To handle involves the skills of playing an instrument as well as manufacturing it. Tubal-cain was a master metalworker and a teacher of the same.

The activities of raising livestock, building cities, creating music and musical instruments, fashioning tools from metal, and cultivating fruits and vegetables are all cultural activities. Culture also involves the attempt to develop political systems, which is what Cain did with the building of the city of Enoch. If fallen man pursues the cultural mandate with such ardor, what then is the task of regenerate man?

Man has been called an inescapably cultural creature. Webster's Encyclopedic Unabridged Dictionary defines culture as the sum total of the ways of living built up by a group of human beings and transmitted from one generation to another; the quality in a person or society that arises from acquaintance with and interest in what is generally regarded as excellent in arts, letters, manners, scholarly pursuits, etc.; development or improvement of the mind by education or training.

Professor James Davidson Hunter in his book Culture Wars distinguishes between private and public culture. Both may be considered realms of symbolic interaction. In private, we deal with symbols and meanings that embrace one's understanding of oneself and one's relationships. Private culture also determines how we process our environment, surroundings and circumstances. How we dress, what we eat, what we read and how we spend our time and money are revealing of private culture. Public culture embraces the symbols and meanings that order the life of a city, region or nation. A nation's laws, the manner in which it limits personal behaviors, its notions of freedom and responsibility and its conceptions of power are all indicators of public culture. Public and private culture should be complementary.

I don't think anyone would argue the fact that America is experiencing cultural wars. How or what one creates in art, business, politics, education, entertainment, literature, science and so on is most assuredly a product of how one sees the world. The fall of man perverted his judgment and sensibility. Some fallen men call good evil, and evil good. They call the ugly beautiful, and the beautiful old-fashioned or outdated. Culture involves standards of truth and beauty. The fall of man was an ethical, covenantal fall. Thereby fallen man tends not to judge culture by ethical standards. He advances the fallen, covenant-breaking culture of the first Adam. Fallen man does not want to have his culture judged by Godly standards.

Just as fallen man does not want to have his culture judged by righteous standards of the Word of God, many Christians have abandoned the cultural or dominion mandate. The fall tarnished man as a culture-builder; redemption restores him. There is still the need to develop skill, to nurture gifts and talents, to train or apprentice, and to understand the specifics of the dominion mandate, the amassing of capital through Godly productivity.

It has been said that the Great Commission is a restatement of the dominion mandate (Genesis 1:26-28; Matthew 28:18-20). When man is redeemed or born-again, some qualitative things occur in him (2 Corinthians 5:17-19; Ephesians 3:20; 4:22-24; Philippians 2:5; Colossians 3:10). Acts 3:21 says:

> Whom the heaven must receive until the times of restitution of all things, which God hath spoken by the mouth of all his holy prophets since the world began.

"Restitution" is the Greek word apokatastasis, meaning to reconstitute in health, home or organization: to restore again. The word describes the reconstitution of the political order, the restoration of property and the returning of hostages to their own cities. Restitution means the restoration (adjustment) to divine favor. Read what God was doing in Jesus Christ in 2 Corinthians 5:19:

> To wit, that God was in Christ, reconciling the world unto himself, not imputing their trespasses unto them; and hath committed unto us the word of reconciliation.

God was reconciling or restoring all things back unto Himself. Restore is the word epilambano, which means to grasp, seize, lay firm hold of; to seize by force, grasp for one-self, to bring into one's sphere. Epilambano means to attain definitively.

Was God successful in His attempt to restore all things?

When Adam and Eve sinned by disobeying God in the garden, legal and covenantal authority over man and the earth passed from Adam to satan. Adam's disobedience and sin caused sin and death to reign in God's creation (Romans 5:17, 19, 21). Satan became the ruler of all those who operate in the sphere of darkness, disobedience and unbelief (Ephesians 2:1, 2; John 8:44; Romans 3:23; Hebrews 2:14-16). It's important to note that satan does not rule the earth! He operates in the realm of darkness, disobedience and rebellion, among those who choose to disobey God and His commandments. He deceives the minds of unbelievers (2 Corinthians 4:3, 4; 10:5).

As long as sin operated in us, it separated us from God and His purposes. As God's enemies, we were under a death sentence (Romans 3:23, 8:7; Ephesians 2:1-3, 11, 12).

However, Jesus paid the penalty for our sin, took our nature upon His sinless self and gave to us the nature of God Almighty (Isaiah 53:3, 4; John 1:29; 2 Corinthians 5:21; Romans 6; Colossians 2:13-15; Hebrews 9:28; 1 John 2:2). When the work of Jesus was completed, He ascended to the Father, and then the Holy Spirit was poured out to dwell in our hearts (John 14:16, 17, 26; 16:7; Romans 8:9). We have been given a new heart (Jeremiah 31:31-33; Ezekiel 36:27). Now we also can have a new mind (Romans 12:2; Ephesians 4:23; Philippians 2:5; 1 Peter 1:22).

God the Father in Jesus Christ the Anointed One came to violently seize you back to Himself for Himself. He came to adjust you and everything about you to the divine favor. And part of this is the restoration of your creative capacities. This does not mean you were unable to create before. As Cornelius Van Til said, it was not that your buzz saw was not sharp, it was that you were cutting at the wrong angle. Now God has restored you as a dominion-minded creative individual.

Dr. Henry Morris, the scientist and president of the Institute for Christian Research, discusses in his Biblical Creationism the prerequisites to created man's dominion. (See Chapter 2, The Dancing Mind.) He goes on to say:

> God said five times that different aspects of His cre
> ation were "good" and then finally, after it was all
> complete, pronounced it all "very good" (Genesis
> 1:31). This divine evaluation could be received and
> then detailed by man in works of music, art and liter

ature, glorifying and praising God for all He had done in creating and making all things.

In the same work, Dr. Morris later states that to be competent to the task of dominion, Adam must have been possessed of "extraordinary intelligence and skill." Morris writes concerning Adam:

> He had come directly from the Creator's hand and was "in His image" – thus surely capable of accurate, rapid analytical reasoning and precise verbal and written communication.

Remember, it was Adam who recorded God's personal account of how the heavens and the earth were created (Genesis 2:4; 5:1). God's revelation to Adam of the natural processes of the conservation and sustenance of the creation were essential to the task of dominion. Adam was totally dependent upon supernatural revelation from God to obey the dominion mandate. Contrary to the musings of modern anthropology, man has not evolved through various stages of lesser to greater development. On the contrary, Adam was created in the image of God and endowed with all the afore-mentioned capacities. Adam and Eve's disobedience in the garden brought death and decay into their lives and dimmed their intellectual and creative forces.

But although their original intellectual and creative forces were dimmed, by the grace of God, their lamps were not completely extinguished. In the Institutes of the Christian Religion, John Calvin writes:

The mind of man though fallen and perverted from its wholeness, is nevertheless clothed and ornamented with God's excellent gifts.

Calvin teaches that each of us possesses a certain aptitude and may manifest talent in some art. In Book II of the Institutes, Calvin writes:

There are at hand energy and ability not only to learn, but also to devise something new in each art or to perfect and polish what one has learned from a predecessor.

Since the Bible teaches that the wise man will increase learning (Proverbs 1:5; 9:9), I am always on the lookout for any materials that will enhance me and those whom the Lord has called me to serve the world over. One gem I have in my personal library is titled Foundations of Christian Scholarship, edited by Dr. Gary North. In Dr. North's introduction, he quotes Langdon Gilkey:

Now Christianity makes the claim to provide the ultimate basis for a meaningful human existence, and it encourages men to find that meaning within the life of culture rather than outside it. It aims among other things, to transform and enrich the enterprise of human civilization... If, then, philosophy joins science, the fine arts, and the economic and political practices of men as one of the essential ingredients of civilization, it is fully incumbent upon the Christian faith to foster a creative philosophy as it is necessary for it to encourage a sound science and a vital art... A healthy Christian culture, therefore, must be able to produce Christian philosophers as well as Christian scientists and businessmen if it is to realize, as it claims to do, the potential goodness of human life.

Create, according to Webster's Encyclopedic Unabridged Dictionary, means to evolve from one's own thought or imagination, as a work of art, an invention, etc.; to make by investing with new functions; to cause things to happen; bring about; arrange as by intention or design; to originate or invent. Creativity is, obviously, the act of creating. Again, in the pure sense of create, man is a secondary creator. However, the task of developing one's creative capacities for the sake of the dominion mandate is critically important.

Unfortunately, many Christians do not believe it to be the role of the Church and of individual Christians to concern themselves with cultural issues. They believe the world – all its nations, cities, peoples and cultures – to be irretrievably lost. They believe the Gospel has the power to save individual souls, but not to leaven cultures and institutions. Individual souls, a few of them, may be saved, but certainly not the cities and nations of the world with all their institutions. Far too many in the Christian Church today believe the Bible only addresses religious issues.

The spirit of anti-intellectualism in the Church today poses a serious threat to the kind of leadership development necessary for the fulfillment of the dominion mandate. We need men in the Church today like Athanasius, Ambrose, Augustine and Calvin – men who brought biblical truth to bear on contemporary issues. Too many of us are staring into space and waiting for the Kingdom of God. Jesus never told anybody to wait for the Kingdom of God (Matthew 4:17; Mark 1:15; Luke 4:43; 17:20).

Jesus told his disciples to pray for the Kingdom to come on the earth as it is in heaven (Matthew 6:9, 10), to seek "first" the Kingdom (Matthew 6:33). Jesus taught that deliverance from sickness and the casting out of demons were signs that the Kingdom of God had come (Matthew 12:22-30, Luke 11:20). He taught that the Kingdom of God comes with great power (Mark 9:1, 1 Corinthians 4:20, Revelation 11:17). The Bible teaches that the reign of Jesus Christ has already begun (Matthew 28:18-20; Luke 10:18, 19; Ephesians 1:17-23; Colossians 1:13; 2:15; Revelation 1:17, 18; 11:15; 19:15, 16; Daniel 2:20-22,44; 4:34; 7:13, 14). Jesus gave His disciples power and authority over sickness and demons (Matthew 10:1; Mark 3:14, 15; Luke 9:1, 2; 10:1, 2, 9, 19).

The Bible teaches that a profoundly transformative work of righteousness has been performed in every believer (2 Corinthians 5:17-21; Colossians 1:9-19; 2:1-10; 3:1-3, 9, 10; Romans 5:1; 8:1, 2; Ephesians 1:7,19-23; 2:1-10; 4:22-24; 5:8; Hebrews 2:10-18; 9:28; 1 John 2:1, 2). We believers have been made kings and priests (Exodus 5:10; 19:6).

As redeemed covenant-keeping believers, we constantly receive the transforming power of the Holy Spirit in and upon us. But the Holy Spirit not only blesses our spirits with His refreshing, He touches our intellects. He breathes upon and restores our imaginative and creative powers. The Holy Spirit infuses us with divine creative ideas. Creativity is not limited to the arts. Whether you are an artist, a farmer, a writer, a scientist, a homemaker, a student, a businessperson, or you are involved in another vocation, you may draw upon the deep reserves of creative potential placed in you by Almighty God.

It has been said that it is not what we are but what we think we are that defines us. That's why it is so important to renew our minds with the Word of God (Proverbs 23:7; Romans 12:2). Many people are discouraged from developing their creative potential by untruths they believe about creativity and creative people. One person may say, "I'm not smart enough." Another may say, "I don't have enough education." These and other excuses fall limp under the mighty power of the Word of God (Philippians 4:13; Matthew 17:20; 19:26; Mark 9:23; Hebrews 11:1, 6; Romans 4:17; 10:17). And excuses such as these have proved untrue in many instances. I have studied the lives of hundreds of creative individuals and read many books on creativity. Many people who became famous for their creative endeavors started dirt poor, with little formal education and in some cases with no parental example of creative achievement to emulate. Some people say too much money, a formal education or too high an I.Q. may hinder the creative process. Whether true or not, many who became successful through the creative use of their talents did not originally aim for success. It was the process and the product they were after. In many cases, success came unexpectedly. Walt Disney, who started his first company with Ub Iwerks at age nineteen, had financial struggles frequently for thirty years. His first venture, the Iwerks Disney Commercial Artists, lasted one month.

Disney, like Albert Einstein, had a father who was a failed entrepreneur. However, genetics have not been established consistently as a significant factor in the creative process. One factor holds true, however: Creative people are dreamers. They are also driven. Most are fueled by childlike imagination.

Another myth of creativity is that it occurs in dramatic bursts of inspiration. On the other hand, most creative work is the fruit of mental, emotional and imaginative toil. The creative so-called genius may be a fairly common person with extraordinarily uncommon drive. Failure does not permanently discourage the creative person. An example is the French military general Napoleon Bonapart, who graduated forty-second out of fifty-eight graduates from Paris' 'Ecole Militaire.

Throughout history, many firstborns achieved great success. The first sixteen astronauts were firstborns. More than fifty percent of U.S. presidents also were firstborns. It's been said that more than half of the most notable leaders and creative people of the Twentieth Century were firstborns. Researchers say firstborns and only children have a better-than-average chance of winning a Nobel Prize. We also know that in the Bible, the firstborn inherited the double portion of his father's wealth and possessions. You may be thinking, But what about me? I'm not a firstborn. But if you are a member of the Church of Jesus Christ, you have the anointing and blessing of the firstborn (Hebrews 12:23). Firstborns are adorned with expectations of great things. They want to distinguish the family name. Just the same, I know you want to distinguish the name of your Father and His family.

Creative people also love books. Many famous creative people, though they may not have had much formal education, self-educated themselves to the top of their particular field. Creative people also turn adversity into advantage. Creative people develop their talents and the gifts God has given them.

Former Librarian of Congress Daniel Boorstin wrote on this topic. In his book The Creators, he said, "Christianity, turning our eyes to the future, played a leading role in the discovery of our power to create." Looking to the future can be the difference between wealth and poverty, according to R.J. Rushdoony and others, who have associated differences between wealth and poverty with differing conceptions of time. Rushdoony says the wealth-building man is future-oriented and understands that each decision he makes today has implications for tomorrow. He plans his life and anticipates the future.

God gives us the power of creativity, in part so that we may apply it under His law to the natural creation and turn its abundance into useful products. Painter, sculptor and inventor Leonardo DaVinci (1452-1519) became obsessed with learning and knowing how to "see" or perceive. He wrote:

He who loses his sight loses his view of the universe, and is like one interred alive who can still
move about and breathe in his grave. Do you not see
that the eye encompasses the beauty of the whole
world? It is the master of astronomy, it assists
and directs all the arts of man. It sends men forth
to all corners of the earth. It reigns over the various departments of mathematics, and all its sciences
are the most infallible. It has measured the distance
and size of the stars; has discovered the elements and
the nature thereof. ... It has created architecture and
perspective, and lastly the divine art of painting.
  O, thou most excellent of all God's creations! What
hymns can do justice to thy nobility; what peoples,
what tongues, sufficiently describe thine
achievements?

As DaVinci notes, there is a strong relationship
between sight and creativity. Jesus said when a person is born
again, he or she is enabled to "see" the Kingdom of God (John
3:3). "See" in this verse is the Greek word eido (i-do), meaning to perceive or have knowledge of; to know, understand, be
aware of. The word eidos (i-dos) means to view; form, fashion, shape, sight. When Jesus was teaching on the Kingdom
of God in Matthew 13, He talked about "seeing" (vv.13-17).
In Mark 4:12, Jesus mentions "seeing" while teaching on the
Kingdom. Being born again, literally re-gened in Greek,
brings about a new way of seeing. Inasmuch as the Kingdom
of God encompasses much more than "religious" things, the
"seeing" brought about by being born again has to relate to
more than the conversion experience.

Jesus healed many blind people in the Bible (Matthew 9:27-30; Mark 8:22-36; Luke 18:35-43). Though these were healings of literal physical blindness, the Bible speaks of a spiritual blindness (Isaiah 6:10; 42:18, 19; Matthew 15:14; Mark 3:5; Romans 11:25.) This blindness refers to spiritual ignorance or lack of discernment. Fallen man cannot "see" or perceive the realities of God's all-encompassing Kingdom. When man has been restored to a right relationship with God through Jesus Christ, he may again receive revelation knowledge through the Scriptures and through the operation of the gifts of the Holy Spirit.

Jesus restores our sight and says that to enter the Kingdom of God, we must become as little children (Matthew 18:3). The average three-year-old has a more active and imaginative mind than the average forty-year-old. This is because children are fascinated by just about everything in their world—new colors, sights, sounds, shapes, faces, textures and so on. And they often learn new things through play. Yes, play. You may be thinking: But play is not spiritual! Doesn't the Bible say put away foolish things? Yes, but joy, laughter, worship, celebration and good, clean fun are not foolish, and neither is creative play. Not only are they not foolish, they are restorative. Some Christians have not laughed since they joined the Church. This is not good, considering the Bible says, "A merry heart doeth good like a medicine: but a broken spirit drieth the bones" (Proverbs 17:22).

Every area where creativity is needed is a province of the Church. In the Gothic period (the Thirteenth to Fifteenth centuries), the cathedral was the most important building in many parts of Europe. This reveals the fact that the dominant worldview presupposed the existence of God. And the cathedral demonstrated the spirit of master craftsmanship in stone-cutting, sculpting, mortar-making, masonry, carpentry, blacksmithing roofing and glass-making. Each of these craftsmen operated a workshop for his own particular trade. There was voluntary cooperation and exchange between the craftsmen. They made all the tools themselves, drew the plans for the cathedral, then began the building process. It could take up to two or three generations to complete the cathedral. Sometimes work had to be postponed because money ran out or because they encountered technical problems. However, the people possessed the spirit of work and knew they were working for the Lord Himself. Therefore, when completed, the cathedral dominated the landscape and told of the glory of God. It was a theological statement usually constructed in the shape of the cross.

Gary North has written to today's potential pastor who is to build a structure: "Construction costs per square foot should not be the primary factor in constructing every place of worship. An eschatology of victory should be reflected in an architecture of majesty and permanence" (North, Tools of Dominion, ICE, 1990). As we study the Bible's comprehensive message of dominion, we must develop ministry that reflects the triumph of Christ over satan. I believe our places of worship should reflect what John Ruskin has referred to as the Seven Lamps of Architecture. They are: sacrifice, truth, power (legitimate power from on High), beauty, life, memory and obedience (to God and His righteous commandments and statutes). Ruskin distinguishes between mere building and architecture. He says "Architecture is an exalting discipline that must dignify and ennoble public life."

According to Alfred Edersheim, the high priests of the Herodian dynasty were creative men. They were woodcutters, carpenters, shoemakers, tailors, sandal-makers, smiths, potters, builders and so on. The Temple at Jerusalem kept a large number of workmen under its employ. The synagogue supported guilds, or associations of tradesmen or merchants organized to maintain standards of excellence and to protect the interests of members. A guild would support out-of-work craftsmen until they found work. Jerusalem's workmen were famous for their artistic skill and creativity.

Rushdoony, noting that the family is the basic economic unit in the Bible, has lamented the loss of apprenticeship. This is the basic intergenerational passing on of skill or craftsmanship, keeping the creative anointing in the family through mentorship and so on. In medieval times, an apprentice would live with the family of the master craftsman. Also during medieval times, the Church was intertwined with the life of the community. It established the purpose for the community. No city institutions were separated from the Church. Even the guilds of creative craftsmen, who saw their purpose as being non-religious, were under the authority of the Church. They built cathedrals and schools. However, later, the university replaced the guild. And this over time contributed to the secularization of work.

During medieval times, sometime around Easter, the city's people would celebrate their creative gifts, talents and achievements with a processional. The city's goldsmiths, painters, carpenters, sailors, leather workers, bakers, clothmakers and every other creative craftsman would dress their best. They would line up in procession with the ministers and procession through the city to the cathedral for worship. This was an attempt to unify the social order. The Church embraced the various ways in which men and women, through their gifts of creativity, sought to minister life to the city.

Like the people of those times, we should seek to consecrate all our God-given gifts, talents and creative capacities to the Lord and ask Him to use them in ministry to our cities. This would be powerful. After all, the creative enterprise for the Christian is a statement of faith in life. It is a rejection of purposelessness and despair.

Let us recapture the spirit of creativity in the Church. Let us accept and develop our gifts, then bring them to the feet of the Master, Who Himself was a creative Craftsman. Jesus' earthly occupation is described as tekton, translated architect, producer, master craftsman.

We need skill to be masters at anything. Choose your domain, and find the best teacher under whom to apprentice. Be patient and learn the craft, whether it's bread-baking or architecture. We need Christian cinematographers to make wholesome yet excellently made, thought-provoking movies. Not only that, we need highly skilled Christian men and women in every area of creative endeavor. God has promised to bless the works of our hands (Psalm 1). He has given us the power, or resources, to obtain wealth (Deuteronomy 8:18). Well-developed creative capacity is a resource, and God has given it to us to help us get the wealth it takes to establish His covenant.

7

THE FIRE OF INVENTION

T he practice of this art of making tools, implements and mechanical devices has never ceased to exert the profoundest influence on the rise of man, and the appearance of this implement-making ability in human life completely transformed man's situation. ... To no small extent the story of man's career is one of the conquest of material resources by means of highly varied devices, tools, implements and machinery.—James Henry Breasted

The everyday world in which we live is shaped by the twin powers of invention and technology. It is the same twin forces that have led to the development of civilization and which drive history forward. All around us are the marvels of invention and technology. The book you are holding is the product of thousands of years of refining paper-making and binding. The ink on this page once would have been crushed ore and charcoal mixed with spittle and animal fat. Now the ink is made from the ground ash of a carbon bearing fuel suspended in a rapidly evaporating solvent. Long ago, you would have been reading the text perhaps off an animal skin parchment, a Nile reed papyrus or a Sumerian clay tablet.

Every year, people extract about fifteen billion tons of raw materials from the earth out of which they fashion every conceivable thing from synthetic rubber to plastic milk jugs to computer parts to toys. Because of research in the area of metal fatigue, we may understand the elastic limit of materials that go into the manufacture of commercial and military aircraft. Even as far back as 1400 B.C., the Greek Daedalus of Athens is thought to have invented a flight machine. He constructed a set of wings, which he strapped to his shoulders and began to flap. For a few seconds, he left the ground. The fire had been started.

We are told that in one notebook alone, Leonardo Da Vinci left about 35,000 words and 500 sketches on flight and proposed machines that would duplicate birds in flight. And the fire of flight in the field of flight as well as in other areas has not been extinguished in man.

An invention is the creation of something that did not exist before. It could be a new and simple gadget, a process, a new material or a complicated machine. Invention is the fruit of man's drive to master his environment. And, as with creativity, this drive, starting with Adam, was instilled in man by God the Creator.

In the informative book Being God's Partner, Rabbi Jeffrey K. Salkin writes:

Adam was made in the divine image. He was given
the task of procreating and dominating the earth. In
the words of Rabbi Joseph B. Soloveitchik, Adam -
who is us - is creative, enamored of technology, and
seeks dignity by mastering and transforming nature.
He is a problem solver and an entrepreneur, aggressive
and bold. He builds, plants, harvests, regulates rivers,
heals the sick and governs. Every time he steps back
and looks at what he has accomplished, he imitates
God Who evaluated the divine handiwork at the end
of each stage of the creation.

Rabbi Salkin teaches us that in the Jewish conception,
it is believed that since we are created in the image of God,
we participate in the act of creating. In the Midrash, God is
called an architect. His blueprint for the creation was the
Torah. Today, builders, designers and architects are said to be
imitating God when plying the creative dimensions of their
own domains. We are told in Scripture that Jesus Christ
Himself was an architect The Greek word is tekton, and it
more accurately translates architect than carpenter. Jesus
Himself was trained to transform the raw materials of nature
into useful tools; a house is a very useful tool.

Architecture is a form of engineering. Duke
University professor Henry Petroski has defined engineering
as "the art of rearranging the materials and forces of nature."
He further informs us that "the immutable laws of nature are
forever constraining the engineer as to how those arrange-
ments can or cannot be made." Invention and engineering are
similar, if not synonymous, processes.

Since the early days of human existence, man has been an inventor/engineer. Petrosky is correct when he asserts that "To Engineer Is Human." I believe that this desire to fashion, fabricate, engineer, create, innovate or invent something is fundamental to the very nature of man. It is the vestige of the image of God.

In his book The History of Invention, Trevor I. Williams wrote, "Civilization has many facets, but how man lives depends very much on what he can make." What man makes is determined by his knowledge of his environment, and his knowledge of his environment is fueled by curiosity. Ultimately, what man makes in part is determined by how curious he is. The systematic exploration of the created order, the physical universe, is science. Science seeks through this systematic study to ascertain the laws of the universe. And technology is applied science.

Technology, which is driven by invention, allowed for the organization of societies, which in turn made possible the division of labor, which continues to push the technological envelope, ultimately giving birth to capitalism. Technology provides support by inventing tools and other things that allow the arts to flower, whether providing instruments for the musician or building theaters for the thespian.

Much of contemporary Christianity seems to be so cut off from most of life. It is, in many cases, a negation rather than an affirmation of life. On the pews of churches across the Western World are people who are bored with monochromatic Christianity. Churches are filled with unfulfilled people whose lives are not marked by what has come to be known as professional ministry. They will never be pastors, church counselors or elders. Don't misunderstand, pastoring, church counseling and the host of other areas of professional ministry are noble and needed. But they are also crowded. Perhaps if more people were being released into the pursuit and fulfillment of their divine destinies, fewer of them would be in need of counseling.

When I meet people, I am always interested in discovering their passion, what it is they want to do, discover and contribute. I believe in people's dreams. I know God gives great big unbelievable dreams, so when people tell me of the incredible things they are believing God for, I want to believe right along with them. Many in the Church suffer from what I call paradigm blindness and what others have referred to as cognitive dissonance. It means your prejudices, assumptions and presumptions hinder you from seeing certain things, such as your purpose. An improper environment can hurt or destroy your purpose, which requires nurture.

Suppose you attended a worship service that was a symposium on how to release the inventive potential God has placed inside you. Would your paradigm blindness cause you to think, This is not God! Why are these weird people talking about creating and inventing things? They should be telling people about Jesus! When we teach or preach about the divine creative inventive spark in the mind/heart of regenerate man, we are telling people about Jesus.

The new birth releases man into a realm of spiritual power, possibility, insight, and potential technical and engineering prowess concerning which mere religion has no clue. The new birth does not simply produce one-dimensional, creatively neutered robots who, like Pavlov's dogs, simply go through the motions of sometimes shallow religious forms. God's power doesn't just flood our souls, it floods our minds, illuminates our creative darkness, and breathes divine potential within us. Proverbs 20:5 states:

> Counsel in the heart of man is like deep water; but
> a man of understanding will draw it out.

"Counsel" in the Hebrew means purposes, devices and so on. Part of the responsibility of leadership is to sound the depths of followers and help to discover the purposes of God that run deep. The average person tends to pursue that which he or she believes he or she can accomplish with little or no effort. These people probably will never invent anything because the history of invention is full of stories of trial and error. Trial and error requires great patience, which is a fruit of the Holy Spirit. You are not called to be average. That is why you are reading this book. God has deposited something in you that will never yield to the habits of the average.

I feel an incredible sense that my generation needs to impart some very specific things to the generation behind us. We must raise up leadership in every field of endeavor. Pietism and Gnostic Christianity that denies the present redemptive power in the physical realm produces listless, lifeless Christians. They would rather fly away than roll their sleeves up and invest their lives in developing prophetic skill levels in the range of disciplines.

We will never produce the kinds of leadership necessary if we consume all the time of young people with redun-
dant church services, and church-like youth meetings that
simply entertain them and pander to indifference and sloth.
The historical antecedents of Western scientific and inventive achievements are to be found in Protestant theology with
its emphasis on the Theocentric (God-centered), biblical
worldview. Science, engineering and technology are all our
province. So are art and literature. I believe that science and
technology will extend into the realized earthly rule of Jesus
Christ. This will be difficult for some Christians to swallow
because they have bought a theology that tells them they will
be wallowing around in a hippie commune eating grapes and
admiring one another's wings.

The relationship between Protestant values and the
rise of capitalism is no longer disputed. However, there is as
much credible evidence that science and technology in the
West were driven by Protestant and Puritan values.
Sociologist Robert Merton has studied this relationship. In
his book Science and Religion, John Hedley Brooke refers to
Merton's work:

> Merton's thesis was that a godly involvement in the
> affairs of the world would also encourage the growth
> of science. There could be real connections between
> the spiritual injunction to glorify God and a quest
> for knowledge that would not only demonstrate the
> Creator's power but also alleviate suffering. To study
> the book of nature was permissible use of the gift of
> reason that differentiated humanity from the beast.

In the Seventeenth Century, Christians did not run from the study of science but saw science as a tool of dominion. Brooke cites a letter from John Beale to Samuel Hartlib written in the late 1650s:

> Here you must add the discovery of, or dominion over all the works of God; the conversion of stones into metals and back again; of poisons into powerful medicines, of bushes, thorns and thickets into wine and oil, and of all the elements to take such guise as man by divine wisdom commands. (ibid.)

Another quote from Brooke strengthens this case:

> For some Protestant thinkers, experimental science promised a way of reversing the effects of the original curse, a way of making a better world that might in some small way mirror the perfection of God's heavenly kingdom, a way of restoring the world to a condition fit for Christ's earthly rule. (ibid.)

To support this, many of the pioneers of science were committed Christians. Men such as Kepler, Pascal, Newton, Farraday and George Washington Carver were all Christians. Many other eminent scientific names were Bible-believing creationists. This list would include such luminaries as Lister, Pasteur, chemistry founder Robert Boyle, James Clerk Maxwell, Mendel, Agassiz, Brewster and so on. Sir Isaac Newton (1642-1721) described the operation of the force of gravity in mathematical terms. He also ascribed the force of gravity to an omnipotent God. Boyle even believed scientific inquiry to be a form of worship.

Science and technology play an indisputable role in shaping the future. That is why it is so important to study and understand them from the perspective of God's Word. Futurist Ron Sellers, in an article in the January/February 1998 issue of The Futurist magazine, says two trends that will definitely affect the future are: (1) increasing clashes between religion and science, and (2) increasing cooperation between religion and science. In the natural realm as new technologies in energy, the environment, farming and food, information, manufacturing, smart materials, medicine, space and transformation reshape the world, it is important that those with vision and understanding of the Kingdom of God ponder these things and seek the Word of the Lord.

We need to understand what is going on in our world in order that we might prosper. As Christians, children of the Kingdom, we have a covenant of prosperity with God (Deuteronomy 8:18; Proverbs 10:22; 13:22; 2 Corinthians 9:6-11). Abraham, Isaac, Jacob, Job, Zaccheus, Joseph of Arimethea and Jesus prospered in the economies of their day. We will do the same. It has been said that technologies in these five areas will be the keys to sustained economic growth in the future:

1) Computers
2) Telecommunications
3) Biotechnology
4) Energy
5) Nanotechnology

Despite the fact that farm labor decreased by 75% and crop land by 10% between 1960 and 1992, farm productivity practically doubled. This in large part is due to better-educated farmers taking advantage of technological advances in agricultural research and labor-saving machinery. Currently, research is being conducted at Georgia Tech in Atlanta with six-inch robotic flying insects that will, among other things, kill harmful insects that damage crops.

Between 1950 and 1990, the sheer computing power of computers increased by eleven degrees of magnitude. Harvard scientist Owen Gingerich says the increase in raw computing power will be the key to advances in astronomy, chemistry, physics, geology, and meteorology.

Already technology has given us synthetic skin, blood and bone. We are told by scientists that they already can make materials that repair themselves, that have the swelling and flexing properties of human muscles. Arguably the most important invention of the twentieth century was the transistor. Microsoft chairman Bill Gates has said without the transistor, the personal computer as we know it today would not exist. The microchip sprang from the transistor, and its presence is almost ubiquitous. Your wrist watch, cellular phone, calculator, computer, television, fax machine, automobile, copier and so on are all possible because of this.

Photonic materials research has made another revolution possible. In information technology, the use of light versus electricity to carry information will produce great changes. Photonics means that instead of being conveyed by electrons in a copper wire, information is carried by photons, or particles of light.

But it doesn't stop there. I could write a book on the technology wave expected to change the world in which we live. Scientists such as Isaac Asimov have envisioned a world where there would be no religion. This world will never come to be. However, the world in which we live will be in many ways different than the present. I have wondered how the Church and her leaders handled secular paradigm shifts, and the religious and intellectual revolutions of their day. How did they handle the proliferation of new technologies and the concomitant religious, social, cultural and economic shifts of their day?

In his book Culture as History, Warren I. Susman suggests, "Each age has its special words, its own vocabulary, its own set of meanings, its particular symbolic order." Susman goes on to inform us that history, ideology, culture and civilization are the key words crucial to social discourse in our time. These are precisely words with which the average Christian does not bother himself or herself. Therefore, we are circumscribed in these matters of public debate. As I understand 1 Chronicles 12:32, the men of Issachar "had understanding of the times." "Times" here means a space of time defined by an associated term, or an age with its own vocabulary. "Understanding" here really needs to be grasped.

The word in Hebrew means to separate mentally; be cunning, diligent, discerning, direct, eloquent, informed, instructed, have intelligence, be prudent, skillful, to teach, to think, (cause, make to get, give, have understanding), to view, to deal wisely.

If we are to have understanding of our times, we must understand the vocabulary, meanings, special words and symbolic order of the age. Robert M. Hazen, professor of earth science at George Mason University and researcher at the Geophysical Laboratory at the Carnegie Institute of Washington, D.C., and his colleague Maxine Singer have formulated what they believe to be the 14 most important questions on today's scientific agenda. They are:

1) What is dark matter?
2) What will be the ultimate fate of the universe?
3) Can we devise a theory of everything?
4) How do atoms combine?
5) Will we run out of energy?
6) What's going on inside the earth?
7) How many people can the earth sustain?
8) How did life on earth originate?
9) Can we unravel the genetic code?
10) How did life on earth become so varied?
11) How do we develop from a single cell?
12) What are the physical origins of memory?
13) Is behavior dictated by genes?
14) Are we alone in the universe?

You may not believe that any of these questions are important for us to answer, but they are. These questions reveal the spirit of the age. They are part of the vocabulary of this epoch of history. The unregenerate man who is asking the questions may not like our well-researched, well-thought-out answers, but that does not allow us to avoid the questions. Lauren H. Seiler, professor of sociology at the City University of New York, has asked, "How long will the human race survive?" He also has expressed an interest in what impact technology will have on our survival. Questions are being asked in every field from the so-called natural sciences to sociology, economics, political science and social psychology. Can science, invention and technology answer all these questions and provide us with an ever-increasing standard of comfort and abundance? Some secular "prophets" are prophesying a technological millennium where science will answer all our questions and resolve all our dilemmas. However, those of us who know the Bible to be the Word of God understand that there will be no technological millennium. We know that there is the millennial reign of Christ, the King of kings and the Lord of lords.

But science and technology in the next century will have enormous implications for the wealth of nations. No longer will that nation endowed with the abundance of natural resources or possessing huge amounts of capital be the wealthiest. This is echoed by such people as MIT economist Lester Thurow, who has presaged that, "In the coming century brain power and imagination, invention and the organization of new technologies are the key ingredients." In 1990, the Japanese Ministry of International Trade and Industry listed these technologies as some of those that will provide the impetus for prosperity and wealth development in the Twenty-first Century:

Microelectronics
Biotechnology
The new material science industries
Telecommunications
Civilian aircraft manufacturing
Machine tools and robots
Computers (hardware and software)

Furthermore, theoretical physicist Michio Kaku in his book Visions cites three important revolutions: the quantum revolution, the computer revolution, and the biomolecular revolution. Kaku cites 1925 as the birth year of quantum theory, which, according to Kaku, had given us "an almost complete description of matter..." This helps us to reduce our understanding of matter to a few postulates and to better understand energy. Kaku says in the coming century, our understanding of matter will allow us to "manipulate and choreograph new forms of matter, almost at will." As for the computer revolution, Kaku says plentiful microchips will lead to the dispersal of "intelligent systems" throughout our environments. Finally, in the biomolecular revolution, Kaku informs that by the year 2025, the human genome will have been decoded, giving us an "owner's manual" for a human being. Kaku says the advance of science and technology in the biomolecular revolution will "give us the nearly godlike ability to manipulate life almost at will."

Where will the children of the Kingdom of God be during Kaku's revolutions? The Bible says God so loved the world that He gave His only begotten Son, that whosoever believeth in Him should not perish but have everlasting life. This includes all the scenario-planners and prophets of the would-be technological millennium. God loves them, and Christ died for them. The Gospel is for them. The children of the Kingdom of God are to be the stewards of the earth. The gospel that was powerful enough to captivate the minds of some of the greatest scientists ever has not lost one iota of its power. Satan wants us to believe that the scientific and technological communities are a lost cause. But satan is a grand liar. We must raise up prophetic leadership to sit at the table with those who would fashion a technological world without God. We must preach His love, but also His judgment.

We must raise up a generation of technologically and scientifically skilled and literate people. We must release the fire of invention in the Kingdom of God. I believe that the loving Creator and Father wants to bless the world with things we have not begun to imagine. But He wants to do it through His people. God wants to reveal things through a people who worship and adore Him. A people who know Him to be the Sovereign Creator of all that is and ever will be. A people who know that invention and discovery are possible because of the great gifts of intelligence, curiosity, rational thought and an orderly universe that God gives to us. All man's revolutions will never give him any more than God already has given.

It is expected that the technological revolution will release great wells of potential in man; however, while technology may assist man in carrying out his tasks, God is the great Liberator of potential.

Authors and futurists Alvin and Heidi Toffler have broken history down into three invention- and technology-driven waves. The first wave was the agricultural revolution; the second wave was the Industrial Revolution; the third wave is the computer revolution. The first wave, according to the Tofflers, took thousands of years to play itself out. The second wave took three hundred years, and the third wave will play itself out in merely decades. In agriculture, the development of the metal plow, along with experiments with other machines, crop rotation, seed and fertilizers, were all systematically pursued. In the Industrial Revolution, the invention of the steam engine, a cheap and easily controlled source of power, made it no longer necessary to locate industrial works on mountain streams, where dams and water wheels could supply power to move the machinery.

The invention of a process for smelting iron with oke in 1709 also helped to speed along the Industrial Revolution. The construction of roads and canals was also important to this revolution. In the middle of the Eighteenth Century, engineers John Macadam and Thomas Telford invented the all-weather road. They discovered that a raised road bed covered with gravel generally could assure year-round passage for vehicles. Later, mining and metallurgy also were discovered during the Industrial Revolution.

Beginning in the 1960s, the computer revolution has altered our lives radically. The computers of today may be traced back to the "calculators" of ancient Babylon. What probably began as roughly piles of numbers with place values of ones, tens and hundreds technologically evolved into the abacus. During the Seventeenth and Eighteenth centuries, scientists and inventors created a number of tools to make the task of calculating easier. For example, in 1642, the Christian mathematician and philosopher Blaise Pascal invented an adding machine to assist his tax collector.

By 1880, because the United States had such mountains of information to process, necessity once again gave birth to invention. In 1884, a young engineer named Herman Hollerith, who worked for the U.S. Census Bureau, applied for a patent on a new statistics-compiling technology. Hollerith's technological offering was a punchcard system that allowed the Census Bureau to keep data on each individual on a separate card. A hole in a specific place on the punchcard represented a particular fact about that person. An electric machine also invented by Hollerith could count the number of holes representing a certain group sorted by place of birth or age.

Subsequent research uncovered ways to make Hollerith's punchcards more useful. The early Hollerith machines could simply sort and count. But by the 1930s, advanced versions of the machines could do mathematical calculations. Then this punchcard machine turned out to be the ancestor of the computer. Later work by men such as MIT's Vannevar Bush, Harvard's Howard Aiken and Bell Laboratories' George Stibitz facilitated the transitional stages between Hollerith's machine and the computer. In fact, a machine built by Stibitz and used by Bell between 1940 and 1949 served as the basis for a machine built for the military during World War II.

World War II sparked an intensive effort to build larger, faster, more complex computers. The result was ENIAC. ENIAC was thirty feet by thirty feet, used eighteen thousand vacuum tubes, fifteen hundred relays, six thousand switches and hundreds of plugwires for programming. It consumed 174,000 watts of power and weighed thirty tons. ENIAC could compute one thousand times faster than any existing machine. It could add five thousand ten-digit numbers in one second. However, ENIAC did not contain a small percentage of the computing power of the six-pound laptop computer I am using to write this book.

Most of us would acknowledge the computer to be a complex group of technologies. However, it has not always been the complex invention that has exerted an enormous impact upon history. One example of this would be the stirrup. The history of the use of the horse in battle may be divided into three periods: that of the charioteer, that of the mounted warrior who clings to his horse by the pressure of his knees, and that of the warrior equipped with stirrups. The invention of the stirrup revolutionized mounted warfare. Before the stirrup, the rider was always precariously mounted, and the use of his weapons was not maximally efficient. The invention of the stirrup made a completely different kind of strategy possible. The stirrup stabilized the rider. The warrior could then place his lance at rest between his upper arm and body and charge with the combined weight of himself and the animal providing the thrust for the weapon. It has been conjectured by some that the stirrup was key to Charles Martel's victory over the Saracens at the Battle of Tours in 732. The significance of this battle is that it decisively checked the

Arab conquest of Western Europe. Edward Creasy in his classic Fifteen Decisive Battles of the World writes that Martel's victory, "...rescued Christendom from Islam, preserved the relics of ancient and the germs of modern civilization..."

Ultimately, we know that the will of God won the day; however, it was a technological development that gave a decided advantage to Martel's troops. The Word of God promises that wisdom dwells with prudence and gives knowledge of witty inventions (Proverbs 8:12). Inventions here means plans, purposes, devices, sagacity, discretion. Also, the word chishshabown (khish-shaw-bone) is the Hebrew for "invent." It means a contrivance, a mental invention, a machine or engine. The feminine form of this word is chashabnah (khash-ab-naw), meaning inventiveness.

Salvation expands man's mental capacity exponentially. There is nothing wrong with being curious about things. As Christians, there is an anointing on our lives to generate solutions to the questions that perplex men and nations. God has placed an inventiveness within us. It needs to be fanned into flames. Inventor Charles Kettering, the pioneer of the industrial research department at General Motors who discovered ethyl gasoline, the efficient ignition system and dozens of items that made the automobile safer, more comfortable and longer-lasting, believed the world was not yet finished. He believed that it is a "God-given dissatisfaction" that drives creative men to seek new footholds.

Unfortunately, not nearly enough of us have ever been mentored in the art of discovery. I agree with Kettering, who found education with its emphasis on grades and tests to exert a negative effect upon a child's willingness to experiment and try. Kettering pointed out that in the classroom, not knowing the right answer meant failure for the student. He pointed out that a scientist/inventor may spend most of his or her life in the laboratory not knowing the right answer. Author Gladys Zehnpfennig in her biography of Kettering (T.S. Denison & Co. Inc., 1962) writes, "Education was synonymous with curiosity in Kettering's mind. He marveled at the wealth of unanswered questions that the universe presented to humanity. If only people would stir their imaginations enough to see that vast panorama through his eyes." Zehnpfennig continues by stating that many people are content not doing so: "Kettering recognized that the average person's mind is too comfortably shackled to small patterns of conformity and that some educational attitudes were responsible."

Kettering believed that education taught us to fear failure. However, the fire of invention does not fear failure. The inventor has to be willing to get it wrong maybe hundreds of times before he gets it right. This is not a trait that most people have developed. A few more of Kettering's related insights also are valuable. Kettering said, "An inventor is a man who does not take his education too seriously." He said people should not become panicky over IQ tests. He said, "If Thomas A. Edison, the Wright brothers and Henry Ford had taken IQ tests, they wouldn't have gotten in the bleachers, let alone the grandstand."

Kettering believed that IQ tests had nothing to do with the person being tested, but with what someone else thought he or she ought to be. He said, "The person taking the test is what he is; he is what the Lord made him." Therefore, people should not become upset when so-called social scientists write books allegedly documenting the "intellectual inferiority" of blacks or any other group. Performance may be measured, but not potential. We are what God has made us, and He hasn't made any junk. And what you are capable of is not determined by what you have done or by what your parents have or haven't done.

The inventor and entrepreneur R.G. LeTourneau, who invented the great earth-moving tractors and machines that were so key to the industrialization of America, had only a seventh-grade education. But he had a God-given curiosity about how things worked, and this propelled him to success in the field of technology. Fifty percent of the U.S. government's contracts for giant earth-moving machines during WWII were awarded to LeTourneau. That was quite an achievement for a man with a seventh-grade education. LeTourneau attributed all his success to God Almighty. Many Christians have not thought that they were to thrive in science, in the inventive spirit, in business or other areas. They are wrong.

George Washington Carver, who achieved international fame as an agricultural chemist, painter and scholar, attributed all his inventions and discoveries to the Great Creator. God gave this man more than three hundred discoveries from the peanut, 118 from the sweet potato, as well as many discoveries from the soybean. Carver's discoveries include cosmetics, facial powder, lotion, shaving cream, cold cream, printer's ink, salad oil, rubbing oil, instant coffee, leather stains, paints and nontoxic colors. He was visited at Tuskegee Institute by Vice President Calvin Coolidge and later by President Franklin Roosevelt. Carver became adviser and confidant to scientists and leaders from all over the world, including Thomas A. Edison and Mahatma Gandhi. Dr. Carver saw his scientific work as the purpose of God for his life. During a speech at Tuskegee Institute in 1928, Dr. Carver said, "purpose alone must be God's purpose, to increase the welfare and happiness of His people. Nature will not permit a vacuum. It will be filled with something. Human need is really a great spiritual vacuum which God seeks to fill." Dr. Carver saw the meeting of human need as a spiritual endeavor. He saw science, invention and discovery as a way to fill human need and to testify to the goodness of Almighty God.

Historian Ernst Benz has written that "the founders of modern technology have felt that the justification of the most far-reaching aims of their technological efforts could be found in this very thought of the destiny of man as imago dei (the image of God) and his vocation as the fellow worker of God...to co-operate with God in the establishment of His Kingdom...to share God's dominion over the earth." The great Church father St. Augustine wrote in The City of God, "There have been discovered and perfected by the natural genius of man, innumerable arts and skills which minister not only to the necessities of life but also to human enjoyment" (1 Timothy 6:17).

The Cistercian, Benedictine and Franciscan monks, who have been credited with the flowering of technology in post-Carolingian Europe, saw their development in what they termed the "useful arts" as part of their spiritual worship and service to God. The Twelfth Century Cistercians incorporated the latest technology—water-powered machinery, water-mills, windmills, metal-forging and ore-crushing devices as well as the skills of machine design, metal-casting, enameling, painting, glass-making, wire-drawing, coin-making, jewelry-making and weapon-making—into their daily lives. These technologies proved very useful in the rebuilding of their abbey at Clairvaux.

All this is important because many secular prophets are prophesying a great golden age when technology will usher in a millennium. They are predicting that science and technology will solve all our problems. It will do no such thing. Once again there is a prophetic void where the Church of the Lord Jesus Christ abandons the realm of technology. But we know that legitimate science and technology are God's gifts to man, and they must be appropriately stewarded and given proper biblical oversight.

Community-based organizations are using technology in an effort to spur economic development in America's inner cities. Computers, software and other technologies are being used to train the poor in skills in demand by world-class companies. The Church should be taking the lead in these kinds of ventures. This is a prophetic time for the inventive spirit to be released in the people of God. As cities across America struggle to develop new strategies in the face of downturns in public funding, the Church must release her creative, inventive and entrepreneurial fires.

The Holy Spirit is longing to release inventions to the Church. Inventions are ideas, ideas that are turned into products, strategies, businesses and sometimes industries. We must become involved in the technological dialogue. We must bring the humility and balance so desperately needed. As children of the Kingdom, we are under no delusion about a so-called technological millennium. We know that this world was created by God and that He is its undisputed Sovereign. We know that God has given us capacious minds and the desire to create, invent and innovate as a reflection of His divine image.

In Exodus 31, we find something rich concerning the filling of the Spirit and craftsmanship. Verses 1-6 state:

> And the Lord said to Moses, "See, I have called by name Bezalel son of Uri, the son of Hur, of the tribe of Judah. And I have filled him with the Spirit of God, in wisdom and ability, in understanding and intelligence, and in knowledge, and in all kinds of craftsmanship. To devise skillful works, to work in gold, and in silver, and in bronze, and in cutting of stones for setting, and in carving of wood, to work in all kinds of craftsmanship. And behold, I have appointed with him Aholiab son of Ahisimach, of the tribe of Dan; and to all who are wisehearted have I given wisdom and ability" (Amplified Bible).

Moses states this in Exodus 35:30-35:

And Moses said to the Israelites, "See, the Lord called by name Bezalel son of Uri, the son of Hur, of the tribe of Judah; And He has filled him with the Spirit of God, with ability and wisdom, with intelligence and understanding, and with knowledge and all crafts-manship, To devise artistic designs, to work in gold, silver, and bronze, in cutting of stones for setting, and in carving of wood, for work in every skilled craft. And God has put into Bezalel's heart that he may teach, both he and Aholiab son of Ahisimach, of the tribe of Dan. He has filled them with wisdom of heart and ability to do all manner of craftsmanship, of the engraver, of the skillful workman, of the embroiderer in blue, purple, and scarlet stuff and in fine linen, and of the weaver, even of those who do or design any skilled work" (Amplified).

Bezalel and Aholiab were filled with the Spirit of God. They were anointed with divine ability to do all manner of craftsmanship. Words such as made, wrought, fashioned and overlaid are used more than fifty times to describe the work of Bezalel and Aholiab. Had Israel had an Office of Patents, Bezalel and Aholiab would have held some fifty-three patents just relative to the Tabernacle of Moses. All the designs, fabrications and so on were by the Spirit of God. The Bible says they were filled with ability, wisdom, intelligence, understanding and knowledge. Bezalel's name in Hebrew means in the shadow of God, or under His divine protection. Aholiab's name means tabernacle of my father. "Filled" is the Hebrew word mala (maw-law). It means to accomplish, confirm, consecrate, fulfill, flow, furnish, have wholly, replenish. This was a replenishing anointing. Now is the time for five-fold ministries in the Body of Christ to lay hands upon the children of the Kingdom to release the Bezalel and Aholiab anointing.

Years ago, visionary animator, entrepreneur and empire-builder Walt Disney left $28 million to found an art school. He wanted to see a community where artists and musicians lived and trained together. That school, the California Institute of the Arts, exists today in Valencia, just north of Los Angeles. Suppose the Church of Jesus were to found and endow the Kingdom of God Institute of Invention and Innovation. It would recapture technology and submit it to biblical principles.

I do not believe we are going to reach the world in which we live with what I call theoretical Christianity. We must have prophetic and incarnational Christianity, meaning revelation must take on flesh and become recognizable to the world. When we build, create, invent, innovate and implement by the Spirit of God, that is incarnational. There are solutions to problems the world faces locked inside the saints of God. These solutions must be drawn out.

Stoking the fire of invention is essential for the development of economic strength in America's inner cities. This is because poverty of material resources is always in some way tied to poverty of inner resources, e.g., ideas, inventions, innovations, products, services. But the mere proclamation of biblical truth is pre-incarnational. Now truth must become incarnational. African-American leaders and parents must teach the rich history of invention, innovation and entrepreneurship that are part of our legacy. It is important to know names and contributions of black inventors such as Andrew Beard (railway coupling), Granville T. Woods (air brake, electric railroad), Richard Spikes, Jan Matzeliger (shoe last machine), Norman Rillieux (sugar refiner) and so on. This is important to teach because African-American inventors and scientists in America have been called "hidden contributors." From the golf tee to the locomotive smoke stack to the lawn mower to potato chips to ice cream, African-American inventors have contributed to the expansion of technology in America. Time and space prevent us from rehearsing the exploits of Benjamin Banneker and Lewis Latimer. The period between 1860 and 1900 was an especially fertile time for African-American inventors. The range of gifts and capacities with which God has blessed man must be released in the children of the Kingdom if we are to make an impact on a cynical world that is results-oriented.

Bell, Benz, Dunlop, Edison, Gillette, Goodyear, Kellogg, Singer and Westinghouse. All these company names are familiar, and they all came into existence because of an invention or inventions. (However, note that not all inventions are technological per se. Things such as the corporation, the research laboratory, the assembly line, mass production, the department store, the self-service store, frozen foods, instant coffee, and the coffee house all qualify as inventions too.)

Inasmuch as entire industries may grow around an invention, inventions are potential wealth-builders. In many cases, they are intergenerational wealth-builders. One of the problems in the Church may be that we have encouraged individuals who should have been starting corporations to start churches. Invention is vitally important to the U.S. economy. Inventions also possess the ability to significantly modify culture, as in the case of television and the automobile. The inventor must be an intrepid person. Nine out of ten inventions or services fail or are drawn from the market after losing large sums of money. It also may take an invention years to reach the market. Despite these challenges, it only takes one significant invention to generate untold wealth. Over the last hundred years, the most valuable invention is said to have been the electric light and power generator. Its value in 1996 was $270 billion.

Is there a fire of invention inside you? Do you have an ache, a yearning to tinker, to discover, to fool around with the laws of motion, mechanics, electricity or just to make something? Even democracy and capitalism are inventions. Believe God to stir and shake all that He has deposited in you. We are to occupy until Jesus returns. Who says it is ungodly for the children of the Kingdom to be inventors of tremendous products and services? Who says it would be ungodly for one or more of these products and services to make it to a market, become wildly successful and become an industry, a corporation that will bless generations? God is able to do exceedingly above what we ask or think according to the power at work in us.

In the new millennium, technology is irreversibly changing the world around us. This is especially important to those of us called to prophetic leadership in this millennium.

Futurists tell us that technology is changing the way we think about life and meaning. Technology brings the world closer to us. Technology exponentially increases our ability to grow food. Technology has expanded our power to communicate.

We need technology and the inventive fire to ensure our competitive success among the industrialized nations. U.S. firms have fallen behind other industrialized nations in the past few years, and success in research and development, technology and the inventive fire are essential to recovering a place of dominance. However, research and development must include broad discussions about the potential consequences of new technology. There is in science a phenomena called the law of unintended consequences, which basically states that inevitably there are things that happen that were neither foreseen nor intended. The potential costs of unrestrained technological growth to human life, the environment and our souls must become part of the discussion. May God raise up apostles and prophets of technology, those who understand its history, its positive and negative contributions, and the moral debate surrounding the notion of unrestrained technological growth and so-called scientific progress.

Those whom God may raise up as apostles and prophets of science and technology will gain access through excellence in some field of scientific, inventive and/or technological endeavor. In this case, prayer must be coupled with skill (Proverbs 22:29). In his Evangelical Theology Lectures on Doctrine, the late A. A. Hodge gives us some valuable insight:

The special work of the Holy Ghost in building up this Kingdom is performed in the regeneration and sanctification of individuals through the ministry of the Church. But beyond this the omnipresent Holy Ghost works to the same end, directly and indirectly, in every sphere of nature and human life, causing all historic movements of peoples and nations, of civilization and of science, of political and ecclesiastical societies, to broaden and deepen the foundation and to advance the growth and perfection of His Kingdom.

According to Hodge, science is not a realm in which the Holy Spirit is unconcerned. As a prophetic people of God, we should be concerned and working everywhere God is (2 Corinthians 6:1). Hodge (ibid) writes:

Thus this Kingdom from the beginning and in the whole circle of human history has always been coming. Its coming has been marked by great epochs, when new revelations and new communications of divine power have been imported from without into the current of human history.

This prophetic view teaches us that it is essential to the march of the Kingdom of God that we release the fire of invention. This fire will burn in the inventor himself or herself, the historian of science, the inventor/entrepreneur, the manufacturer, the CEO and so on. All these are ministries that must be released and encouraged in the Body of Christ.

However, it is important to understand that God never intended that we deify technology and the inventive fire, and that technology is not going to solve all the world's problems. We have faster, smarter, readily accessible machines today. However, they have not eliminated hunger, poverty, racism or a host of other seemingly intractable ills that plague the human condition. Technology has not taught us how to convince sixteen-year-old girls not to get pregnant. It has not solved the problems of gangs, drugs or violence. Technology allows us to communicate with our friends in Africa and other parts of the world but does not strengthen our friendships with our next-door neighbors. These are matters of the heart as it were and will never be solved by science and technology. These will be addressed by people whom God has touched and who compassionately touch others. There is a spiritual void in our technologically rich world. It will not be crossed by smart machines, but by people-to-people contact, by the joyful celebration of redemptive purpose, by the worship of the only true and living God Who gives us all things freely to enjoy. While we celebrate the inventive fire that God has placed within us, we do not worship the fire or its products. We must acknowledge the gift He has given to us, work diligently to create and invent, celebrate life, serve humanity and worship God.

8

THE FIRE OF ENTREPRENEURSHIP

The dictionary definition of the entrepreneur is a person who organizes and manages any enterprise, especially a business, usually with considerable initiative and risk; one who takes risks; an employer of productive labor.

John W. Gardner in his book Self-Renewal writes that, "The future is shaped by men and women with a steady, even zestful, confidence that on balance their efforts will not have been in vain. They take failure and defeat not as reason to doubt themselves but as reason to strengthen resolve. Some combination of hope, vitality and indomitability makes them willing to bet their lives on ventures of unknown outcome."

Of course, several other definitions of an entrepreneur exist. Lloyd E. Shefsky says an entrepreneur is one who enters a particular business in time to form or change its nerve center. It does not matter if the person has started the business or what the business is. What matters is that the entrepreneur changes things. And we must use our God-given entrepreneurial fire to do just that.

The intent of this book is not to cite the statistics that establish economic disparities between ethnic groups in America. Much work already has been done in that area, and the mere reciting of statistics would defeat the book's purpose. I believe that far too many people are confused about the difference between statistics (facts) and truth. You may not want to consult the statisticians before you decide to respond to your entrepreneurial fire. They may discourage you by saying you are the wrong color or sex, didn't graduate from the proper schools or won't be able to secure capital. They will tell you how many businesses fail each year and why.

However, what they won't tell you is whether it was the discovery of uncharted lands, the manufacture of new products, or the pioneering of new techniques in the arts and sciences, change always has been made by those who have taken risks. Entrepreneurs have been called the masters of opportunity. The principle is simple: Today's economy is based on innovation, and those who provide breakthrough solutions will find success.

God promises that people who are in covenant with Him are to expect material as well as spiritual success (Genesis 12:1-4; 13:1-6,14-18; 22:14-18; 24:1, 33, 34; 26:12-14,18-22; 28:3, 4; 39:2; Exodus 12:35, 36; Leviticus 25, 26; Numbers 6:24; 14:8, 21, 24; Deuteronomy 1, 2, 3, 4, 6, 7, 8, 24:19; 26, 28; Psalm 1; Proverbs 10:22; 2 Corinthians 9:6-11). God promises in Psalm 1 to bless the works of your hands. This is a reiteration of the promise stated in Deuteronomy 24:19.

Many people have erroneously been taught that the Bible is a book that exalts poverty. Nothing could be further from the truth. In a time when many in the general society are being paralyzed by the hopeless dirges of the statisticians, we need thousands, millions of God's people to respond to the entrepreneurial fire. I am well aware of the disparities in income between various groups in American society. However, many of our black leaders are preaching a kind of statistical determinism. We are consistently told about the intransigent racism that pervades American society and how blacks will never succeed because of it.

We know that racism still exists in America, but it's also important to know that there are golden opportunities to succeed. It is interesting that many of those who scream loudest about America's insuperable racism are themselves testimonies to positive things that may be achieved. Many are tenured professors at Ivy League universities, published authors, television talk-show hosts, popular national and/or international lecturers and speakers and so on. I am not denying that these individuals have experienced racism. But many of them also have achieved imitable levels of success. It is important to know the ingredients of success and failure. What produces failure and what produces success?

You must determine whether you will be lead by those who believe your failure in American society and in the world is inevitable, or by those who still believe that God works in the affairs of men and is committed to your success. If you choose the latter, this does not mean that you will not have to be smarter, work harder and possibly deal with more frustration. But I think any genuinely successful person is smart, hard-working, and knows how to handle frustration. People who do not believe they are smart will not try.

You should understand that God does not tempt and tease you with powerful ideas only to laugh at you and say that your skin color or gender prevent them from ever coming to pass. I fear that many of our leaders today have an intellectualized view of a God distant from contemporary events. They invoke His name in a Machiavellian fashion to solicit popular sentiment but have long ceased to believe that He will really make a way out of no way. Too many of our leaders have bent their ears to the academes and facticians. They preach a gospel of impossibility based on gloom, doom and social determinism. This is distinct from the Gospel of Jesus Christ. The Gospel is a message of hope. I remember a time when we preached that God was hope for the hopeless. The Gospel of Jesus Christ tells us of God's desire to remake us from the inside out, to change our hearts and minds, and to infuse us with the mighty power of the Holy Spirit.

God gives us His life, His Word, His promises and His power. This is real. We must not be lured into worshipping the quasi-secularist's almost powerless God. The question is, How much power do you think your God has? To you, is your God merely a cultural relic with no power to deliver His people? Are you without hope in the world? If so, you should realize that it is a sin for you to go to church, say you worship God and not believe Him when He says that with Him all things are possible. Whether you succeed or fail in life largely will depend on what you choose to believe. Don't secularize God.

Don't allow statistics to destroy your faith. You are not obligated to fail to verify someone's intellectualized and pessimistic worldview. As a Christian, you are never to be limited by data and statistics. The Word of God must be your life compass. The anointing will establish you in life. God is greater than any obstacle you face!

So you have success as a promise of God. Who will you believe — those who say you can or those who say you cannot? You may say, "If you will prove to me that I will succeed, then I will try." I cannot do that. I do not know you. I do not know how hard you are willing to study and work on improving yourself. But I do know that because you are reading this book, there are some things stirring in you and pointing you in the direction of good success (Joshua 1:8). I do know that the Bible is the greatest success book ever written. And I know that just as I cannot guarantee your success, neither can the forecasters of doom guarantee your failure. Sure, they can recite statistics and horror stories. They can give you the facts, but truth will always triumph over facts. There is a spiritual power in the Word of God. It is literally the life of God. No statistics can harness the Word of God. We all want to be the person who does the unthinkable and the impossible. So make yourself available to God, trust Him wholly, and no man will ever be able to predict your failure.

Trade, commerce and business are to be found throughout the Bible. Abraham and Solomon both were international businessmen. Though he concentrated on Palestine, Egypt and Arabia, Abraham's territory as a merchant prince extended from Haran to Egypt. Abraham imported and exported those luxury goods that were exchanged by the rich of all countries. We are told that Haran was a miniature Chicago. Its trade routes extended in all directions. Ur, the city from which God called Abraham, was then the most influential commercial city in the world. The fact that Abraham's ancestors had at least three cities (Serug, Nahor and Terah) named after them suggests that his family was very influential. The reference to Abraham's wife, Sarah, as a "wife-sister" identifies her as a member of the aristocracy of Haran. Abraham controlled the grazing rights between Shechem and Hebron. He invested his money in a variety of enterprises, among them cattle and silver (Genesis 13:2).

Abraham established himself in Gerar, the commercial hub of Palestine Negeb. In so doing, he established a legal base of supplies for Egyptian trade. To the south, Palestine's key commercial partner was Egypt, the greatest civilization of antiquity. Arabia was Palestine's other southern trade neighbor. Samaria and Babylonia were the only great manufacturing civilizations to ever rival Egypt. Abraham's father, Terah, ran trade routes from Ur to Haran. Abraham represented his father from Haran to Egypt through their banking offices in Damascus.

So you see, the father of our faith was a very successful international businessman and banker. To place this revelation concerning Abraham into context, look at the book of Galatians. Galatians 3:13, 14 states:

> Christ has redeemed us from the curse of the law, having become a curse for us (for it is written,

"Cursed is everyone who hangs on a tree"), that the blessing of Abraham might come upon the Gentiles in Christ Jesus, that we might receive the promise of the Spirit through faith (NKJ).

The great business acumen and success that Abraham enjoyed as a blessing from God is also for you and me today. It is part of the blessing of Abraham that Christ's death has made available to us. This is a blessing that we must receive through faith. Abraham, Isaac, Jacob, Job and others in the Bible passed God's very own integrity test. They were great men of God. However, we cannot overlook, spiritualize or allegorize the fact that they were also men of incredible wealth. Much is said in the Bible concerning the wealth of Solomon. God blessed him tremendously. In addition to all his other wealth, he had a monopoly in copper. Solomon was also the nation's leading horse trader, and trading in horses often involved chariots (1 Kings 10:28, 29). Solomon was involved in a lucrative Red Sea trade partnership with Hiram of Tyre (1 Kings 9:26-28; 10:11, 12, 22). At least twenty-five Hebrew root words are translated wealth, riches, prosperity and so on. In the Bible, wealth consisted of flocks and herds, gold, silver, frankincense, clothing, wool, linen dyed purple and embroidered, saddle cloths and oriental rugs. All kinds of precious stones also were considered wealth. Emerald, pearl or agate jewelry was wealth, along with ebony and ivory imported for inlaid furniture. Metals were used in The Old Testament. Gold, silver and copper are mentioned, along with iron, tin and lead.

By the time of the prophet Isaiah, manufacturing became the main source of wealth-building. And manufacturing involves the entrepreneurial fire. There were several successful businessmen in the Bible. David should be mentioned among them. David, as a general in the Army of God, extended his conquests to the Euphrates River. He established an iron monopoly when that metal was in great demand. David's military victories also allowed him to tax any items crossing his borders. Remember, it was David's wealth that built both the Temple and the palace of Solomon. Biblical scholar, commentator and study Bible author Finis Jennings Dake has placed David's contribution to Solomon in gold and silver alone at $100,695,000. He gave much more in brass, iron, wood, precious stones and marble (1 Kings 29:1-5).

In my studies, I have learned that there are two primary pre-conditions for sustained business activity. They are social and economic stability, and surpluses. Jericho, the city the Lord gave to Joshua (Joshua 6), possessed a stable agricultural community, and produced surpluses in crafts, pottery and trade.

Much preaching that has gone on in the Protestant churches has included the unqualified condemnation of wealth-building and business/entrepreneurial success. Through this kind of preaching and theology, I believe that God-fearing people have chosen not to pursue a calling from God in these areas, which is unfortunate. This, however, was not the case with Sir John Templeton, an international investor and philanthropist, who originally desired to become a missionary. Thank God for those who are called to the mission field, but that was not Sir John's calling. This great man, knighted by the Queen of England in 1987, was called to the realm of business and finance. His innovative investment techniques and worldwide philanthropy have blessed many.

In his book Business As A Calling-Work and the Examined Life, scholar and author Michael Novak has made the case that the legitimate pursuit of business/entrepreneurial success is in fact a calling from God. Novak writes:

> Business has a vested interest in virtue. It cannot
> go forward with realism, courage, wisdom, honesty
> and integrity without a highly motivated and virtu-
> ous work community. It cannot endure without lead-
> ers and colleagues in whom the key virtues are inter-
> nalized.In this and many other ways, business is
> dependent on the moral and cultural institutions of
> the free society:

These virtues to which Novak refers are the classic virtues of temperance, fortitude, practical wisdom and justice. Of course, the Bible has its own catalog of virtues (2 Peter 1:5-11). There are eight: faith, virtue, knowledge, self-control, perseverance, godliness, brotherly kindness and love. The number eight in biblical numerology represents new beginnings. Novak teaches that virtue is essential to true business success. It is interesting that in the Petrine text mentioned above, these virtues are being enumerated in conjunction with being diligent to make one's calling—including business and entrepreneurship—sure.

In Greek, the word translated virtue is arete. In Homer's poems, arete refers to excellence of any kind. One may exemplify arete as an athlete, a soldier or a scholar. Courage is one of the virtues, or excellences. In this conception, courage is necessary for the maintenance of a household, a friendship or a community. The courageous one is one who may be relied upon. In addition to courage, physical strength and intelligence are considered to be the heroic virtues, or excellences. And in Homer's Odyssey, prosperity is spoken of as a virtue, or excellence.

There is a misconception that all wealth is ill-gotten. It is not true that every successful entrepreneur is dishonest. This belief in the innate evil of wealth may have kept you from pursuing a calling as an entrepreneur. But the poor have no corner on virtue. Any such notion has no grounding in Scripture. You and I were placed on this earth to prosper, to use our gifts and talents to the maximum. God has given us the power to obtain wealth (Deuteronomy 8:18), and entrepreneurship is one of the ways to obtain it. Novak says the three cardinal virtues of business are creativity, community-building and practical realism, or the capacity to listen, to learn and to be self-critical (Proverbs 13:18).

There is a majestic quote from Pope John Paul II that speaks prophetically to our purposes here. He writes:

> Indeed, besides the earth, man's principal resource is man himself. His intelligence enables him to discover the earth's productive potential and the many ways in which human needs can be satisfied. It is his disciplined work in close collaboration with others that makes possible the creation of even more

extensive work communities which can be relied upon to transform man's natural and human environments. Important virtues are involved in the process, such as diligence, industriousness, prudence in undertaking reasonable risks, reliability and fidelity in interpersonal relationships, as well as courage in carrying out decisions which are difficult and painful but necessary, both for the overall working of a business and in meeting possible setbacks.

God has given you the power to obtain wealth. He has given you the earth with its vast resources (Psalms 115:16; 104:24). He has made His wisdom available to you (1 Corinthians 1:30; James 1:5-8). He has given us His Word and His promises (Deuteronomy 5:28, 29; Isaiah 1:19, 20). He has given you a covenant (Genesis 17:7, 21; Galatians 4:28). He has promised you success (Deuteronomy 24:19; Joshua 1:8; Psalm 1:1-3). He has given you faith (Romans 10:17; 12:3), and He has given you time (Psalm 91:16; Proverbs 3:13-18). All these are keys to entrepreneurial success.

The Bible never condemns the earning of profit. In fact, it encourages profit-making (Matthew 25:14-30; Luke 19:13; Isaiah 48:17). The Hebrew word meaning to profit is ya'al (yaw-al). It means to ascend; to be valuable, be benefited; able to do good. Another Hebrew word translated profit is yithrown (yith-rone), meaning excellence, to exceed, to excel, to abound, an overhanging, excess superiority, wealth, abundance of riches, better, excellency.

Walt Disney was an entrepreneur. He was turned down by banks and suffered much rejection trying to build

Disneyland. But as Disney did, an entrepreneur must learn to endure rejection and to handle failure. A. David Silver says the entrepreneur is energetic, single-minded, and has a mission and a clear vision. Silver writes, "He or she intends to create out of this vision a product or service in a field many have determined is important, to improve the lives of millions." God promised you in Joel 2:28 that He would give dreams and visions. The Bible teaches in Proverbs 29:18 that until people have a vision, a prophetic, redemptive picture from God of the future, they will cast off restraint. The King James version says they will perish. "Perish" means to loosen, expose, dismiss, refuse, uncover. Individuals, families, cities and nations need God-given vision to ward off the loosening and exposure of satan.

The fire of entrepreneurship is fueled by vision. Many of the world's most successful entrepreneurs did not begin with much, but they had a vision. Many were not born with silver spoons in their mouths. They began just as you are, with an idea and a burning passion to help people. Many of them began with the desire to give more to ministries, to bless the Kingdom of God. This is right where David started. He was anointed king as a little shepherd boy. He tells us in Psalm 122:9 of a big prayer he prayed, then he worked hard, trusted God, developed his gifts and talents, and accepted the varying levels of responsibility that God sent his way. You know the end of the story. David lived the latter years of his life as a very rich man. But he started off simply wanting to bless the house of God.

Many ministers today separate religion and this type of entrepreneurial vision. Because of this, one evangelical CEO is reported to have said, "I would tell more ministers to get out of ministry than I would tell businessmen to get out of business." Dorothy L. Sayers once wrote:

> In nothing has the Church so lost her hold on reality as in her failure to understand and respect the secular vocation. She has allowed work and religion to become separate departments, and is astonished to find that, as a result, the secular work of the world is attuned to purely selfish and destructive ends, and that the greater part of the world's intelligent workers have become irreligious, or at least, uninterested in religion.

Why should people be interested in a Christianity that does not concern itself with their daily lives and work? They shouldn't. Biblical Christianity has a prophetic word for the workplace, the stock market, the boardroom, the undergraduate business curriculum and the master's in business administration (MBA) program. Christianity has a prophetic word concerning leadership and management, resource procurement, investment, charity and philanthropy. I am believing God to raise up apostles, prophets and prophetesses with the entrepreneurial fire raging inside them.

One of the things that will bring renewal to America's urban communities is the unleashing of this entrepreneurial fire through the Church. When we study African-American history, we find a rich and enduring legacy of entrepreneurship, all the way back to Anthony Johnson, the first African-American to become an entrepreneur in the New World.

Johnson arrived in America before the Pilgrims did. He owned property in Jamestown, Virginia. He was followed by merchant, wholesaler and some say founder of the city of Chicago, Jean Baptist DuSable.

Prior to the Civil War, not all African-Americans were slaves. Those who were not accumulated capital and started small businesses. Concerning these free blacks, professor John Sibley Butler wrote:

> Indeed, these African-Americans developed enterprises in almost every area of the business community prior to the Civil War, including merchandising, real estate, manufacturing, construction trades, transportation and extractive industries. This underscores the fact that Afro-Americans are woven historically into the economic fabric of America and cannot be looked upon, in totality, as a recently arrived ethnic group. (John Sibley Butler, State University of New York, 1991)

Like these African-Americans, entrepreneurs are not people who sit around waiting until everything is perfect before they make their move. Entrepreneurs are people of action; they like to make things happen. They don't wait for permission before they act. Entrepreneurs enjoy finding solutions to problems. They love to find new ways of doing things. Entrepreneurs are never satisfied with their current success. Entrepreneurs do not create new products, services or ways of doing things for the money. They create because they have to. The money comes when they find better ways of doing things.

Entrepreneurs are people of faith, and they want to be self-employed.

In the United States, firms with 100 to 500 employees represent the fastest-growing segment of the economy. When governments create an entrepreneurial environment, it fosters the growth of small business. Countries such as Japan and Germany have realized the value of promoting an environment in which small businesses can thrive.

Certain cultural factors also help determine who may become an entrepreneur. If your parents owned or own a business, you are more likely to become an entrepreneur than if they were salaried employees. Also, your propensity for risk-taking is a factor in determining whether you become an entrepreneur.
John G. Burch has given nine character traits you need to possess as an entrepreneur:

- A desire to achieve.
- Hard working.
- Nurturing. An entrepreneur can birth and nurture a project until it can stand on its own.
- Acceptance of responsibility.
- Reward orientation.
- Optimism.
- Orientation to excellence.
- Organization.
- Profit orientation.

Entrepreneurs create new human opportunities. They

develop new technologies and organizations. Entrepreneurs add wealth and value to the general society. Entrepreneurs discern and pursue opportunities. Entrepreneurs are inveterate learners. They know what they do not know, and they find ways to learn it. The entrepreneur learns and studies his or her potential market. Entrepreneurship has been called a practice, meaning one learns the theory, then applies it repeatedly. The entrepreneur is made, not born. The entrepreneur is not afraid of those who know more and have more experience than he or she has. As the Bible says, "The wise man is glad to be instructed..." (Proverbs 10:8). It has been said that every economy depends on entrepreneurs for survival. The creativity and energy of these entrepreneurs prevent an economy from being destroyed by ever new circumstances.

Some visionary Church leaders have recognized this and have begun to teach and promote entrepreneurship in their churches and ministries. This is important. The Church must do this. America has been a land of entrepreneurs since the beginning. The early expeditions here were investments in the possibility of finding wealth for the investors in the New World. The Jamestown Company, the East India Company and the Massachusetts Bay Company were all examples of this entrepreneurial thrust into the New World. To thrive, these companies needed investment capital, managers and products that were useful locally first and then exportable. One of the things entrepreneurs do is create new markets for their products and services.

It is difficult, however, for groups displaying certain patterns of social pathology to produce entrepreneurs. The entrepreneurial ethos tends not to flourish in communities where there is not an emphasis on the requisite virtues. Single-parent families, drug and alcohol addiction, high crime rates, out-of-wedlock pregnancies, dependence upon the government, a scarcity of existing prosperous enterprises, a disrespect for elders, history and positive tradition, a decline of the Church's ethical influence, and a decline in educational achievement hinder the growth spark of the entrepreneurial fire. In communities where these pathologies persist, the comprehensive preaching and teaching of the Gospel of the Kingdom of God is the only lasting curative. I strongly encourage an interface between churches, businesses and government agencies when that is appropriate.

Again, I believe God is raising up apostles and prophets of entrepreneurship, not simply to be examples of ethical financial success, but to teach the principles of entrepreneurship, and to stoke the fires of entrepreneurship in the Church of Jesus Christ. The Bible says, "...The wealth of the sinner is laid up for the just" (Proverbs 13:22).

One of the most important elements in stoking the fire of entrepreneurship is intellectual capital.

Thomas A. Stewart has defined intellectual capital as the "intellectual material - knowledge, information, intellectual property, experience - that can be put to use to create wealth," (Intellectual Wealth - The New Wealth of Organizations, Thomas A. Stewart, Doubleday 1997).

In the age in which we live, wealth is considered to be the product of knowledge. Stewart says knowledge is more valuable than the physical assets that are used to constitute wealth. Things such as natural resources, physical plants and big bankrolls are seen today to be less important than the intellectual assets of an organization.

While vacationing in Hawaii a few years ago, I found an interesting book, If You Want to Be Happy & Rich Don't Go to School, by Robert T. Kiyosaki. Kiyosaki says in the book that in our society, an understanding of money is "absolutely required." He says given the structure of our modern society, neglecting to teach these skills of understanding money is tantamount to not teaching the skills of farming in an agricultural society.

It also is important to understand that mistakes will occur along the road to entrepreneurial success. Our educational system teaches that it is not desirable to make mistakes. It often teaches that there is only one way of doing things. This is anathema to the entrepreneur. Some of the world's most successful people have been some of its most notorious mistake-makers. You must have the ability to make mistakes, to learn from them, and to rebound and remain focused on what you are committed to achieving.

Entrepreneur, consultant and author Art Mortell's book The Courage to Fail should be read by everyone who believes they have a destiny of achievement. He writes that success is based on failing most of the time. Mortell, whose book is a college course on mastering the fear of failure, gives practical tools for dealing with the phenomenon of failure. He says, "We resolve resentment by conquering our fears." He also says, "If we cannot accept failure, we will quickly lose our enthusiasm."

Entrepreneurial success is never an accident. It is the result of the mastery of certain principles, vision, hard work, constant learning, building networks of relationships and never giving up. People who do not have adequate and healthy confidence in their intellectual capital probably will not try to make it as entrepreneurs. This is a two-sided coin; too much, as well as not enough, knowledge can paralyze your efforts. There is obviously a balance to be struck.

William J. Hudson, in his book Intellectual Capital, tells us that courage is what drives growth in intellectual capital. Remember, courage was one of the virtues of the heroic society. Hudson states that we need courage to use our intellects and to generate brilliant ideas. He says it takes courage to balance an emotional situation with reason and logic.

Reason and logic are not un-biblical. God reveals Himself as a God of reason (Isaiah 1:18). The Hebrew word for reason is yakach (yaw-kahh). It means to argue, decide, correct, convince, plead or prove. Jesus is revealed by John as the Word of God (John 1:1-5, 14). The Greek word for Word is logos, which also means logic. God is reasonable and reasons, Jesus is logic, so it is perfectly consistent with their natures to act both reasonably and logically. And you will need both of these to succeed as an entrepreneur. Mastery of the knowledge of a specific domain is essential to the experience of releasing your ultimate potential.

If you are called to be an entrepreneur, you must know your product or service. If there is an existing market, you must know it thoroughly. If not, you must understand market forces and how to create your market. Study the art and science of entrepreneurship. You must know the habits of your customers. You must be a lifelong learner. And above all, you must give God the glory for all your success. The wealth you accrue must be used to bless people. You must be a tither and a generous giver into the Kingdom of God. And you must be willing to teach others what you have learned, using your God-given time, talent, treasure and influence to light the fire of entrepreneurship in others, leading them on the trail to multi-generational entrepreneurial success.

9

THE FIRE OF THE ARTS

Professor George M. Marsden of Notre Dame University has reminded us that the natural and supernatural realms are not sealed off from each other. The reality of God revealing Himself in Christ is called the incarnation. Incarnation is what happens when the supernatural of God manifests itself in and among the natural of man. It is the spiritual and the natural touching. In his book The Outrageous Idea of Christian Scholarship, Marsden writes, "The incarnational motif also has implications for the arts, humanities and social sciences. It suggests, for instance, that we may see God working in the ordinary, if we only have the eyes to see. Poets, artists and musicians may be most open to giving expression to such dimensions of reality, but they are there for all to perceive."

An earlier chapter discussed creativity. However, this chapter deals specifically with the arts—music, literature, painting, sculpture, dance and the dramatic arts, in particular. I am not discussing the arts as the purview of a particular economic or intellectual elite. Nor do I discuss them as mere appendages to man's real existential situation. I discuss the arts in a real sense that music, painting, poetry, sculpture, dance, literature and cinema can convey powerful humanizing truth that enables and empowers us! After all, flourishing in the arts is yet another dimension of the dominion mandate.

Pitirim Sorokin, an astute Russian scholar and author, has written that, "The fine arts are one of the most sensitive mirrors of society and culture of which they are an important part."

In his book The Sensate Culture, professor Harold Brown offers powerful insight on this subject:

> The arts reflect the fundamental orientation of
> society as well as the particular views and behavior
> patterns of its members; at the same time, they
> spread and reinforce such views and patterns. All
> of the arts in the west, including popular art and
> its extreme forms, are becoming increasingly chaotic
> and disoriented, and in this respect they both reflect
> and intensify the chaotic and disorienting tendencies
> in society and culture. In short, when we understand
> what is going on in the world of art today, we shall
> understand a great deal about the present condition
> and the probable future of our late sensate socio-
> cultural system. (H.O.J. Brown, Word, 1996).

The socio-cultural system is the web of human relations along with the myths, ideologies, theological, anthropological, legal and historic-chronologic presuppositions that provide their support. Art is the prism through which our philosophy and morals are refracted. The arts are not morally, intellectually or creatively neutral. When urine, feces and human sex organs become "art," we have a problem with eroding sensibilities. The goal of art is not simply unchecked expression. I agree that the refined products of culture, literature and the fine arts should tend to uplift the general culture (Brown, Word, 1996). Brown writes that "the higher forms of art, music, literature and theater should have a moral, educational and edifying impact on the general public."

Just what constitutes the "higher forms of art" is debatable within certain parameters. For instance, I don't know that professor Brown has listened to John Coltrane or Wynton Marsalis. I don't know whether he has read Toni Morrison, Ralph Ellison, Richard Wright, James Baldwin, Langston Hughes or Countee Cullen. I believe these artists are all part of what constitutes the "higher forms of art." There is a swelling in my chest when I listen to Yo-Yo Ma play Bach's Cello Suites. I appreciate Bach's compositional genius to the degree that my layman's understanding allows. I am somehow enlarged by the prodigious musicianship, interpretive passion and democratic spirit of Yo-Yo Ma. When he plays "Libertango," there is a respect for not just Astor Piazzolla, but for the tradition from which the music comes.

When I listen to Wynton Marsalis, whether it be Citi Movement, Blood on the Fields, In This House on This Morning, something happens at another level. In part it is his unquestionable musicological genius. He is also interpreting some of what I know to be my own history and that of my ancestors. My bosom swells again. Musicians paint with their instruments as painters with their brushes. With Yo-Yo I see; with Wynton I see.

Perhaps some think that as a Christian, I should not listen to Yo-Yo Ma or Wynton Marsalis. Maybe they think these men are "worldly" musicians. I don't know whether either of them are Christians, and maybe their music isn't expressly Christian. Maybe it's even secular. However, there is a distinction to be made between the secular and the profane, and this music is anything but profane.

Sidney Finkelstein in his book How Music Expresses Ideas offers this observation on what music offers:

> Music is not simply made by following one tone with another, but by a succession of tones which the ear grasps as a unit, like a melodic phrase or a melody. These units are "human images," for they evoke states of life. Larger forms are created involving complex melodic chains, alternation and variation of melodies, simultaneous interplay of two or more melodic lines or "polyphony," formations of "chords" or groups of different notes that, struck simultaneously, merge to sound like a single note with an enriched "feeling tone." Such complex forms evoke psychological states that are "human portraits." Through such "human images" an "portraits" music can be and said to embody ideas. (Sidney Walter Finkelstein, International Publishers, 1970)

The embodiment of ideas in music explains the existence of national and ethnic music. The national anthem of a nation should ideally embody the ideas, aspirations and myths of that people. There is perhaps no clearer historical example of this than the relationship between the German composer Richard Wagner, the philosophy of Aryanism and the ideology of Nazism. Wagner believed the world could be redeemed through the philosophy of Aryanism. Wagner's ideas have been called an "outright gift to the Holocaust." German novelist Thomas Mann (1875-1955) wrote that he found an element of Nazism in Wagner's literature, music and creative work. The German philosopher Friedrich Nietzsche also was greatly influenced by Wagner. This is significant because of the influence that Nietzscheanism has exerted upon the Twentieth Century. Nietzsche scholar and biographer Walter Kaufmann writes of the scope of his influence:

> Nietzsche, more than any other philosopher of the past hundred years, represents a major historical event. His ideas are of concern not only to the members of one nation or community, nor alone to philosophers, but to men everywhere, and they have had repercussions in recent history and literature as well as in psychology and religious thought. (Nietzsche: Philosopher, Psychologist, Antichrist; Walter Kaufmann, Princeton, 1974)

Nietzsche has been said to have presaged Darwin, Freud, Kant and Rousseau. Nietzsche's "superman" came to be identified with German nationalistic ideas, his will to power with German militarism and imperialism. Needless to say, Adolf Hitler, also profoundly influenced by Wagner, was among Nietzsche's chief devotees.

The underlying philosophy of Wagner's work has been referred to as hedonistic libertarianism. This philosophy of the Young German Movement rejected the "inhibitions" of so-called bourgeois morality, favoring natural freedom and sensual indulgence. Wagner was a proponent of the French Revolution and a virulent anti-semite. Wagner's work so expresses these ideas that to this day on those infrequent occasions when his music is played in Israel, it is met with public protest.

Of the ideas the music embodies through its human images and portraits Finkelstein has this to say:

> These are not the ideas that may be found in a scientific tract but commentaries on a society showing what it means to live in it. They embrace developments in sensitivity, in the human's awareness of his own powers, and in the situation of internal freedom, as conditions change in the external world. In this way music joins the other arts in creating social consciousness, or the individual's awareness of the internal life he shares with society, and in revealing the internal history of society. Music also brings to bear upon the education of the present, past growth in sensitivity and freedom.
> (Finkelstein, International Publishers, 1952)

Our study of the arts is prophetically significant. The Bible says God was in Christ reconciling (restoring) all things back to Himself (2 Corinthians 5:19). Restoration is a recurring theme in the biblical prophetic writings. The Greek word for reconciliation is katallage (kat-al-lag-ay). It means to restore to divine favor. A Hebrew word for restore is shalam (shaw-lam). It means to be safe in mind or body; to be completed, finished, full; peace, prosperity, recompense; to completely restore, deliver, finish; health, welfare, prosperity. Another Hebrew word for restore is alah (aw-law). It means to mount up, excel, ascend, to break the day, shoot forth, spring up, stir up, cause to burn, exalt, increase. In 2 Corinthians 5:18, the Bible says we have been given the ministry of reconciliation. Remember the use of the term "the world" in 2 Corinthians 5:18. "World" here is cosmos (kosmos), or orderly arrangement, adorning, to take care of, provide for. The ministry of reconciliation connotes our stewardship over the earth. Thus, there is a prophetic message of the restoration of the arts to the Divine Favor of God.

The late C.S. Lewis reminds us that, "In the earliest times theology, science, history, fiction, singing, instrumental music and dancing were all a single activity." This says the arts have a specific social function. Restoration is inescapably incarnational and social in its application. Music being a medium through which we communicate human images and portraits and an embodiment of ideas, it becomes a channel for the message of restoration to the Divine Favor of God not just to the Church but to the broader culture. We need people in the Kingdom of God who have a musicological anointing. I believe we have limited the range of musical expression in some of our circles. Every legitimate art form is to be restored. Jazz, classical, country, rhythm and blues, and so on can come under the anointing. But will it then be called Christian music? Not necessarily. Is it expressly biblical lyrical content that defines a piece of music as Christian? If so, then all instrumental music would be by definition excluded.

Christian musicians desiring to push the envelope of musical expression and to reach a broader audience should know that it is not a sin to want to reach people through the musical gift God has given them. This quote from Finkelstein, which applies to any artist, not just the musician, reveals the impact of art:

> Aesthetic emotion, or recognition of beauty, aroused by its concrete state, is central to the arts, including music, and marks the difference between art and life. The aesthetic emotion is a special kind of joy. It is a reaction to a leap in knowledge of the kind that transforms the human being by opening up new possibilities of life. (ibid.)

Notice some of the evocative words in this quote. Words such as "special kind of joy," "leap in knowledge," "transforms" and "new possibilities." Have you thought of your artistic gift in these terms? Do those of you who write, compose music, paint, sculpt, act and so on approach the art in terms of its potential to open "new possibilities of life" and to facilitate "a leap in knowledge"? In what fresh new ways can the fire of the arts propel us to excellence in form, composition and presentation?

Johann Sebastian Bach (1685-1750) said his purpose in life was to create "well-regulated church music to the glory of God." He was an inveterate learner possessed of a titanic work ethic. Such musical giants as Bach, Handel, Beethoven, Dvorak and Stravinsky remind us that artistic mediocrity is in no way to be associated with Christianity.

Our artistic responsibilities are not limited to music. The late French existentialist philosopher and writer Jean-Paul Sartre talked about the relationship between music and literature. He wrote, "There is no doubt that the arts of a period mutually influence each other and are conditioned by the same social factors" (Jean-Paul Sartre, What Is Literature?, 1949). When the various artists in the artistic community look at the contemporary socio-cultural situation, what do they see? It is an interpretive question, a matter of understanding the signs of the times. The artist should not merely record the raw facts of what is "there." The redeemed artist who understands the ministry of restoration should look to convey, to prophesy through his or her artistic gift. When we begin to study literature, we see the relationship between music and the spoken word.

Sir Arthur Quiller-Couch has defined literature as "a record of memorable speech; it preserves in words a record of such thoughts or of such deeds as we deem worth preserving." In ancient Greece, the poetry of Homer was recited to the accompaniment of the lyre. Quiller-Couch has defined verse (poetry) to be a record in metre and rhythm. Prose, he says, abhors metre, "uses rhythm laxly, preferring it to be various and unconstrained, so always that it convey a certain pleasure to the ear." To read works of certain prose writers is akin to listening to a jazz composition or studying an abstract painting. When I read Herman Melville, author of Moby Dick, there is an elegance and fluidity of language and a depth of meanings that compels me to grapple with the meaning of the text and its possible underlying meanings.

In C.S. Lewis' letters to Arthur Greeves dated August 1930, he points out the purpose of some to write:

> I am sure that some are born to write as trees
> are born to bear leaves: for these, writing is a
> necessary mode of their own development. If the
> impulse to write survives the hope of success,
> then one is among these. If not, then the impulse
> was at best only pardonable vanity, and it will
> certainly disappear when the hope is withdrawn.

Lewis also wrote, "Whenever you are fed up with life, start writing: Ink is the great cure for all common ills, as I have found out long ago." Novelist Ralph Ellison once said, "Fiction became the agency of my efforts to answer the questions: Who am I, what am I, how did I come to be? What should I make of the life around me? ... What does American society mean when regarded out of my own eyes, when informed by my own complex sense of the present?" In an essay titled A Very Stern Discipline, Ellison writes that the American writer should "use his imagination to question and penetrate the facade of things."

Some of Ellison's insights on the writing of the novel are akin to Finkelstein's notion of the social formation of music and its embodiment of ideas through assimilating human images and portraits. In his essay The Novel as a Function of American Democracy, Ellison writes:

> The novel is a form which deals with change in
> human personality and human society, bringing
> to the surface those values, patterns of conduct
> dilemmas, psychological and technological, which

abide within the human predicament. It can abstract, from the flow and fury of existence, these patterns, which are abiding, and re-create them in the forms of artistic models that can be controlled and imbued with the personal values of the writer, even down to the last punctuation mark. In other words, the novel is a way of possessing life, slowing it down, and giving it the writer's own sense of values in a delicately and subtly structured way.

All this, of course, is not simply a matter of entertaining, but is a way of confronting reality, the nature of the soul and the nature of society. As a form, the novel permits the writer to survive the consequences of encountering the chaos he must reckon with when he attempts to deal with the basic truths of human existence.

Author and professor Elie Weisel wrote:

To write is to plumb the unfathomable depths of being. Writing lies within the domain of mystery. The space between any two words is vast than the distance between heaven and earth. To bridge it you must close your eyes and leap. A Hasidic tradition tells us that in the Torah the white spaces, too, are God-given. Ultimately, to write is an act of faith.

In his book The Writer as Social Seer, Robert N. Wilson writes:

Literature should, then, be regarded as a field in which the nature of man may be richly explored. ... Resulting from the individuals of a society, it indicates certain things about them and their forms of group behavior. Acting upon the reader, literary works are a shaping force in personality development and social organization. The arts and the artist are central, not peripheral, to any informed cognizance of human motives or actions.

Wilson also writes:

A society's common values are reinforced, and some times revised, through the medium of art. If the writer restates the accepted values of a group, and does so in an appealing, convincing fashion, his work shores up the existing system. It may confirm the members of the society in their traditional ways of behaving.
(Robert N. Wilson, The Writer as Social Seer, UNC Press, 1979)

We've seen the dramatic social function of art in society. Because the arts do have such a valuable social function, the philosophical tastes, morals and general worldview of the artist is critically important. Again, "good" art seeks to make us better. Art must avoid the bourgeois trap of becoming the province of elites within society. All the people within a given society must have the opportunity to express themselves artistically, and to be taken seriously by the larger culture. The various members of multi-peopled societies such as our own must be encouraged in organic artistic expression. What is the dialogue like between the artistic ethos professed by a nation and that of its various citizens?

If the Church of Jesus Christ is going to have anything credible to say to the so-called secular world, it will have to learn to seriously use the medium of the arts. The work of people such as Patrich Kavanaugh and the Christian

Performing Arts Fellowship is significant and needs to be duplicated many times.

As we encourage people in the pursuit of their God-given purpose, the doors of possibility to expression in the arts must be part of what is considered. God wants His children in the arts. It is my humble opinion that He wants musicians, not just popular ones, but classical and jazz musicians. Coltrane practiced his horn up to eighteen hours a day. You probably don't have that kind of time to practice. But that being the case, apart from the supernatural intervention of God, you should never expect to attain a voice comparable to the genius from North Carolina. I believe God wants writers who will seek to learn the art of writing good fiction that reminds man of what is possible in a post-nihilistic society.

The writer must study language, word usage, symbols, myth and allegory. Michel Foucalt (foo-kō) and Noam Chomsky have discussed the relationship between language, power and freedom. The statement that knowledge is power has been traced to Foucalt. While he is incorrect in his asser-tion that there is no absolute truth, he is correct in analyzing the relationship between knowledge and the power of certain groups in history to impose their conception of truth and morality on others. This is called "constructing truth." Foucalt says the "truth" coming from the social sciences (he refers to them as the human sciences) allows people to decide matters that define humanity and affect people in general. If enough people can be persuaded to what the scientists have decided to be truth, then according to Foucalt, then it may seem to be more important than other, unknown truth.

For instance, when the book the Bell Curve was published, it was purportedly an objective scientific study based solely on an analysis of the data. Past performance provided data for the study. The problem with this is that though past performance may be evaluated and analyzed by certain criteria, potential is not subject to the measurements and analysis of social scientists. Again, the problem is that if enough people are persuaded to adopt the "truth" of the Bell Curve studies as their own, this "truth" claims at the time to be more important than the inapparent truth of potential and purpose.

In Problems of Knowledge and Freedom, Chomsky writes:

Industrial civilization leads to the concentration of power and the decline of individual liberty, but at the same time it frees men from the worst forms of servitude, the burden of stupefying labour, and makes it possible to imagine a world of free men who will achieve the "liberation of the creative impulse" that is the true end of social reconstruction.

I would augment Chomsky's conception of social reconstruction by stating that conceptions of social reconstruction may never be based upon the philosophy of relativism. Atheistic humanism cannot be the basis of law and politics in our conception of social reconstruction. We must avoid the veritable rearranging of the Titanic's deck chairs.

Prophetic art must deal with power and its relationships with knowledge. Prophetic art must deal with the Foucaltian notion of the power to create belief; the power to decide what is knowledge in the first place, and the prerogative of claiming to know more than the rest of us. This is particularly relevant in an age when only "facts" verifiable via scientific method may make claims of "truth and knowledge."

Poet Ezra Pound has written that literature has to do with the clarity and vigor of thought and opinion. It has to do with the solidity and validity of words. Pound intones that the reader is only moved by clarity and efficiency of language. Pound writes, "Great literature is simply language charged with meaning to the utmost degree possible."

George Santayana wrote: "Language habitually wrests its subject matter in some measure from its real context and transfers it to a represented and secondary world, the world of logic and reflection." Santayana biographer John McCormick writes: "Music makes narrative possible; without music, speech would be equivalent to algebra or shorthand." Reason is prominent in the process, for "Language vitiates the experience it expresses, but thereby makes the burden of one moment relevant to that of another. ... To turn events into ideas is the function of literature."

Santayana believed that the writer's art is half genius and half fidelity. He warned the writer that to rely on inspiration alone would lead one astray. He wrote of the writer: "His art is relative to something other than its own formal impulse; it comes to clarify the real world, not to encumber it."

Whether the arts should be part of an educational curriculum has sparked debate. I believe they should. Abraham Maslow believes they should. In his book The Farther Reaches of Human Nature, he wrote, "Education through art may be especially important, not so much for turning out artists or art products as for turning out better people." How does art begin to succeed in this function of turning out better people? Art for expression's sake can never accomplish this task, for it disdains the very notion of taste, reason, nobility and the heroic upon which good and great art must be founded. Presbyterian minister Dr. D. James Kennedy wrote, "Jesus Christ has given art its loftiest themes. ... Many of the greatest masterpieces in the world have had a Christian theme or base."

This is very interesting. Western civilization is based upon the worldview of the Bible. Its cultures mostly have been developed upon biblical themes. Its art, music and poetry primarily have been contributed by Europeans. The music of Bach, Handel and Beethoven. The painting of Rembrandt, Michelangelo, van der Goes and Gauguin. The literature of Dante, Shakespeare, Whitman, Faulkner and Melville are all part of what constitutes fine art and high culture in the Western world. And this is as it should be. All these artists are teachers, and we can learn from them all.

However, we need to know that there is rich artistic tradition that flows from pen, brush and instrument of non-European cultures. Much of this art is fused with the ethos of struggle—struggle against the oppressive structures of race, economics, and politics. It's art that seeks to confer dignity upon people who may have been denied it.

Elie Weisel has said that to write is an act of faith. Generally speaking, the contemporary context provides the themes the writer will address. The artist, in this case the writer, so immerses himself/herself in understanding the times in which he or she lives. You may be thinking, But doesn't the

Bible say to love not the world, neither the things that are in the world? Doesn't the Bible say that if you love the world, the love of the Father is not in you? The Bible does say these things.

However, when the Bible speaks of not loving the world, it is referencing the fallen systems of knowledge, politics, economics, art, religion, the socio-cultural milieu of an age. The orderly arrangement of the cosmos as God originally intended is another matter. Becoming immersed in understanding one's times is not tantamount to loving those times. We must understand the various strategies through which satan attempts to captivate the minds of men, cities and nations. Inasmuch as the artist is an agent of social transformation, we need to call forth those artistically gifted in the Kingdom of God, train them to think biblically and prophetically, then release them into the world and the Church to minister.

Kingdom artists must learn to discern artistic trends and fads. They must be taught to discern the philosophic underpinnings of art works. Where is a particular artist coming from in his/her work? What does his or her use of color, light, tonal variations, rhythm, harmony, space and language suggest morally and philosophically? This means there must be apostolic and prophetic leadership in the Church to mentor and train Kingdom artists. The creative realm of the Holy Spirit is infinitely more vast than what we perhaps have recognized. How can the artistic envelope be pushed to find creative and distinct ways to communicate the restorative truth of God? What is the Word of the Lord to the arts community? In the Church of Jesus Christ, we must raise up artists who can translate the Gospel of the Kingdom into artistic expression with a passion for excellence and a commitment to form and craft.

There may be a Bach, a Beethoven, a Coltrane or a Marsalis sitting next to you in church this Sunday. Or there may be a Shakespeare, a Melville, a Hughes, a Wheatley or a Baldwin. Someone in your youth or children's ministry may be the next great painter, sculptor or architect. The New Birth is the beginning of a process of spiritual recreation. We go from faith to faith, from glory to glory, from strength to strength. It is not simply an ethereal realm of the spirit that is being recreated or restored. All that you were intended to be is being restored. Your relationship with the loving Creator Who is our Father, your gift of wisdom, your intelligence, your creativity, your innovativeness, your entrepreneurship and your inventive spirit are all products of God's great work of restoration.

The expanse of European art is at least in part common knowledge. Most Americans know who Beethoven is even if they have never heard any of his music. Many Americans know that Herman Melville wrote Moby Dick even if they have never read it. Most people know the name Michelangelo even if they know nothing about him. The genius of African-American art and artists is a generally lesser-known fact. The eminent W.E.B. DuBois wrote that the African-American is primarily an artist. Not only does a substantial and significant corpus of work by African-American artists stand on its own, it is impossible to talk of American art, especially literature, music and theater, without noting the distinct contribution of African-Americans. DuBois writes:

> From the earliest times the presence of the black man in America has inspired American writers. Among the early Colonial writers the Negro was a subject as, for instance, in Samuel Sewall's Selling of Joseph, the first American anti-slavery tract, published in 1700. But we especially see the influence of the Negro's condition in the work of the masters of the Nineteenth Century, like Ralph Waldo Emerson, John Greenleaf Whittier, James Russell Lowell, Walt Whitman, Julia Ward Howe, Harriet Beecher Stowe and Lydia Maria Child. ... One must remember that it would be inconceivable to have an American literature, even that written by white men, and not have the Negro as a subject.

> (The Oxford W.E.B. DuBois Reader, Edited by Eric J. Sundquist, Oxford University Press, 1996)

He writes:

You cannot discuss religion, morals, politics, social life, science, earth or sky, God or devil without touching the Negro.

DuBois asks the question, "Would America have been America without her Negro people?" (The Souls of Black Folk, Modern Library, 1996)

Eric J. Sundquist the author of a book titled To Wake the Nations: Race in the Making of American Literature

(Belknap Pr, 1993), writes of DuBois' take. In the book, professor Sundquist writes:

> As DuBois understood, a reconstruction of the "work
> and striving" of American culture was not a matter of
> merely adding a few novels and poems to the tradi-
> tional list of cultural documents but rather of recogniz-
> ing the the degree to which American culture, proper-
> ly read, was already saturated with the black gifts of
> story, song and spirit. It was a matter, that is to say, of
> responding to linguistic structures and modes of
> expression that had long been woven into the funda-
> mental fabric of American culture but that few had
> the ears to hear.

Those having no ears to hear have certain preconceptions of European exclusiveness of American culture. There are certain mythical, ideological, linguistic, style and content prejudices that inform their thinking. The French writer Andre Malraux said, "Artists do not stem from their childhood, but from their conflicts with the achievements of their predecessors; not from their formless world, but from their struggle with the forms which others have imposed on life."

The writer is a reader: a reader of prose, poetry, social and cultural history, biography, literary criticism, newspapers, magazines. The writer reads other contemporary writers, good and bad. The writer is a student of language, style and form. All the great writers were voracious readers.

A Christianity that is afraid of the popular mind will never produce great artists, prophetic artists, who translate the powerful themes that Christ and the Gospel of the Kingdom give to them into images, language and sounds that through the act of creative faith strive to make us better. Think about the forms that have been imposed on life that should and must be challenged by an informed biblical world-view. It is the province of the prophetic artist to discern and challenge these forms.

I confess that I am humbly asking the Church of Jesus Christ to reconsider the general pessimism that pervades most of our preaching and polity. I am asking for a full-blown the-ology of prophetic engagement with all of life and culture. The late Christian author Dorothy Sayers penned what would be part of a manifesto of the theology of prophetic engage-ment. She wrote:

> If the Church is concerned with civilization, or
> with politics and economics, it can only be on
> the grounds of a realistic and sacramental theology
> of the incarnation. For this means that the whole of
> man's humanity, and its most vital, developed and
> characteristic is the vehicle of the divine part of
> his nature. ... A Church which takes up this fully
> sacramental position must not confine her concern
> with civilization to the political and economic aspects
> of civilization. If she undertakes to sanctify humanity,
> it must be the whole of humanity. She must include
> within her sacraments all arts, letters, all labour and all
> learning ... For she stands committed to the assertion
> that all human activity, whether of spirit, mind or
> body, is potentially good - not negatively, by

repression, but positively, and as an act of worship. Further, she must include a proper reverence for the earth and for all material things.

The French philosopher and author Jean-Paul Sartre believed that humans almost never experience what he termed reality. He believed that reality is mediated through institutions. Sartre taught that these institutions camouflage reality. This camouflaged, institutionally mediated reality again deals with the power to create meaning. It deals with man-made structures of language, theories, explanations, traditions, customs, mores and so on. The structures possessing the power to create meaning constitute the dominant culture. David S. Reynolds has written that, "It has become common to view literature as an isolated act of rebellion against a dominant culture."

This is true of the birth of American literature. American literature assimilated and transformed images and devices from an English socio-literary context into its own distinctive voice. In short, the birth of this American literature brakes the cultural hegemony of English prose. In the same way, the birth of African-American literature began to deal with issues of race, freedom and dignity in America. African-Americans began to construct their own images and to challenge the dominant culture's mediated "truth" and "reality" concerning themselves.

While I disagree with much of the thought of men such as Foucalt, Nietzsche, and Sartre, I believe that in the case of Foucalt and Sartre, their analysis of structures of power and the power to create meaning is valuable for the artist seeking to prophetically address those structures. While we glean what is useful from these and other thinkers, for the prophetic artist, the ultimate truth comes from God and His holy Word. The postmodern notion that there is no absolute truth is both Nietzschean and Sartrean, but it is not biblical. Biblically, there is an absolute truth that transcends one's experience (William James), one's anguish (Soren Kierkegaard), one's phenomenological, structuralist or existential plight (Husserl, Saussure, Levi Strauss).

There is an obvious inconsistency in the philosophy of postmodernism. It posits absolutely that there is no absolute truth. All that exists is the nebulous concept of nature. In this philosophy, the material universe is all that exists. Perhaps in the Church we have taken an all-too-over-confident approach to this reality. Most contemporary art is a mirror for the philosophy of postmodernism.

Postmodernism is a secular humanist philosophy. As such it trumpets such notions as free inquiry. According to secular humanist Paul Kurtz, free inquiry includes the "freedom to cultivate and publish the fruits of scientific, philosophical, artistic, literary, moral, and religious freedom." It also posits the separation of church and state, based upon errant interpretations of the U.S. Constitution and of the intent of the founders. Secularism espouses an idea of freedom, an ethics based not on the revelation of God and the Bible, but on what it calls the critical intelligence of man. This is a "moral" conduct based on reason. It is a non-absolutist morality; in other words, it is not universal. Secular humanists claim religious skepticism but value moral education. However, if there is no absolute truth, there can be no absolute moral truth. So how does one provide moral education where there is no universal understanding of what morality is?

It was Nietzsche who posited that God is dead. The Russian writer Tolstoy wrote that if God is dead, anything goes. The humanist suggests there can be morals without God. I do not agree, but our subject matter is primarily and secondarily philosophy. Nietzsche warned us that God is dead, then Sartre came along and set the philosophical world on its head. He taught that instead of essence preceding being, the opposite was true. With God being dead, or having never existed in the first place, there can be no God as a reference point for man. Sartre would say that since there is no God to conceive human nature, then there is no such thing. Since there is no God, there is no idea in God's mind to which humans must correspond. As such, each person creates his or her own essence each moment through his or her choices and actions.

Notice Sartre says humans create their own essences. Philosophically, essence is what a thing is, its definition, nature, function, the idea of the particular thing. So in this conception, humans create their own definitions, meaning, function and so on. Obviously, in this conception, there can be no doctrine of the sinful nature of humans since this revelation comes from God. The non-existence of God leads to an absurd universe. The root of absurd is surd. In Arabic, the surd is a mathematical impossibility. Considering this, the non-existence of God leads to a mathematically impossible universe.

Sartre believed that the cowardly human mind cannot handle the thought of an absurd universe, so it postulated the existence of God to relieve the anguish brought on by the thought of meaninglessness. This is where the transformative power of prophetic art comes into play. The writer, painter, sculptor, composer, playwright or other type of artist seizes upon the raw material of absurdity and meaninglessness and fashions meaning. The early Nineteenth Century African-American writers turned non-human slaves into human beings with dignity, with a voice, seizing upon the choice to begin to redefine themselves and to examine in their own words the nation and the structures and institutions that defined their lives.

Truth and meaning are the persistent concerns of the writer and of the prophetic artist in general. Richard Weaver wrote a valuable book titled Ideas Have Consequences. It is true: In the realms of human knowledge and endeavor, in the practical realms of government, economics, art, international relations, religion and so on, ideas do have consequences. The idea that Christians should not be involved in the arts has netted the consequence of turning the arts over to the philosophies of secular humanism. It has left many artists to toil under the delusion that God is dead and to seek to reconstruct an absurd world using the defective tools of materialist philosophies and the loss of the heroic impulse.

According to Daniel J. Boorstin in the book The Creators, Dostoyevsky believed there to be a relationship between literature and the other fine arts. Dostoyevsky also understood the importance of ideas. According to Boorstin, Dostoyevsky wrote:

by laws which we cannot understand. Ideas are infec-
tious, and an idea which might be thought to be the
prerogative of a highly cultured person can suddenly
alight in the mind of a simple, carefree being and take
possession of him."

Such is the case with the ideas of freedom and liberty.
Such is the idea that men are endowed by their Creator with
certain inalienable rights, rights to life, liberty, and the pursuit of happiness. These ideas in the minds and upon the lips
of patrician orators mean one thing; these ideas in the hearts,
upon the lips and upon the tips of the pens of oppressed men
mean something else.

African-American literature protesting slavery can be
traced back to the first decades of the Nineteenth Century
with the polemic essays of the African Society of Boston.
David Walker's Appeal appears in 1829, and the tradition of
protest literature continues through the 1800s until the present day. Sermons, poems, biographies, slave narratives, political pamphlets, African-American history pamphlets, novels
and social studies informed the African-American literary
corpus.

Some of you may be asking why I, as a Christian writer,
am concerned with secular philosophies and their propo-
nents. Why do I concern myself with Nietzsche, Foucalt,
Sartre and others? It is because I am not a capitulating
Christian. I believe in the Dominion Mandate. I believe that
Christians are the legitimate inheritors of the earth. I do not
subscribe to the assumed primacy of materialist philosophy.

God is not dead. As in a book title by the late prophet Francis A. Schaeffer, He is There and He Is Not Silent. It has not been the thought of Christians that has shaped the modern and postmodern worlds. Nietzsche and Sartre have been called two of the most important philosophers of the Nineteenth and Twentieth centuries. It is their thinking, along with that of Marx, Darwin, Huxley and so on, that comprises the curriculum of the academy. It is their influence that pervades most of contemporary art. According to author, Gary DeMar, we are in the midst of a War of the Worldviews.

Because of this, the artistic fire of the children of the Kingdom must be released to prophesy against the dregs of arrogant humanism, pathetic nihilism and lonely absurdity. We must remind the so-called secularists that even the foundations of their philosophical notions have been constructed from reasonable biblical, theistic postulates. It could be argued that without Christianity, none of these philosophies that fancy themselves to have demolished the theistic worldview would even exist.

This is why the prophetic Christian writer must be as the sons of Issachar in knowing well his or her times. Together, let those of us who aspire to excellence in prophetic artistry learn from our teachers. Both Newton and Einstein acknowledged that they saw further because they stood on the shoulders of those who went before them. In the Church of Jesus Christ, we need wise and excellent practitioners and teachers of style, form, history, craft, voice and much more.

The same that is true in music and literature also is true in painting, sculpture, dance and the dramatic arts.

Painting and sculpture, in particular, are attempts at getting at the world through the medium of sight. They have been described as asking an ever-living question of the world through the visual sense. The visual and dramatic are not without their philosophical presuppositions. Notions of perception, spatiality, depth, dimension, color, form, clarity, materials and so on are very important. The painter, sculptor, dancer or architect is an artist possessing the ability and desire to transform visual perception into material form. To study visual art is to study the history of the various ways in which man has viewed the world.

Painting, sculpture and architecture deal with vision. Like music and literature, the visual arts evoke human images and portraits that come to embody ideas. Sir Herbert Read in A Concise History of Modern Painting gives some interesting insights on vision and seeing as social constructs. He writes:

> We see what we learn to see, and vision becomes a
> habit, a convention, a partial selection of all there
> is to see, and a distorted summary of the rest. We see
> what we want to see, and what we want to see is deter-
> mined, not by the inevitable laws of optics, or even (as
> may be the case in wild animals) by an instinct for sur-
> vival, but by the desire to discover or construct a cred-
> ible world. Art in that way becomes the construction
> of reality.

Rudolph Arnheim has written on the relationship between the visual arts and thought. He stated, "Thinking calls for images, and images contain thought. Therefore, the visual arts are a homeground of visual thinking." Arnheim further wrote, "Thinking requires more than the formation and assignment of concepts. It calls for the unraveling of relations, for the disclosure of elusive structure. Image-making serves to make sense of the world." For Arnheim, "The work of art is an interplay of vision and thought."

The Bible teaches us that as a man thinketh in his heart (mind), so is he. Arnheim says thinking contains images. Therefore, the images that emanate from the thinking of man in artistic form reveal something of who man is, or perceives himself to be.

The Gospel of the Kingdom of God embraces the thought of Henry Van Til in his The Calvinistic Concept of Culture. In this book, Van Til writes:

> One cannot keep on evangelizing the world without
> interfering with the world's culture. ... In Christ
> man is restored to God as cultural creature to serve
> his Maker in the world and as ruler over the world
> for God's sake.

As the worldview set forth by the Bible comes increasingly under attack from postmodernism and scientific utopianism, art having no Truth in which to ground itself will cease to be a voice and will increasingly serve only as an echo. Set adrift from the moorings of taste, aesthetic, intellectual integrity, and the humble, authentic search for truth, art becomes nothing more than visual cacophony.

The late theologian Paul Tillich believed art to be important because it is the chief indicator or barometer of the faith or "ultimate concern" of a generation or culture. (The

Christian, The Arts, and Truth: Frank Gaebelein, Multnomah, 1985) Keith Miller says, "In a real sense I believe God is presented in the Christian revelation as more of a loving and creative artist than as a philosopher or theologian."

The capacity to make and enjoy works of art is a gift of our humanity. G.K. Chesterton said, "Art is the signature of man." The late prophet, brilliant theologian and scholar Francis A. Schaeffer said, "Made in God's image, man was made to be great, he was made to be beautiful, and he was made to be creative in life and art." God, our wonderful loving Father and Creator, made man and placed him in the midst of the inexplicable beauty of His own art. Man was to be surrounded by beauty. Father gave man beautiful things to see, smell, hear, taste, touch and perform. All this in the place of paradise, the Garden of Eden.

God also gave man genius and responsibility, according to a beautiful passage in Frank Gaebelein's book The Christian, The Arts, and Truth:

> Did you ever think of genius as the great cultural phenomenon of God's sovereignty? Through those to whom he has given genius he graciously enriches human life. With a fine impartiality he gives genius and talent as he wills in all fields, of course, not just in the arts, and to all kinds of people. But always human responsibility accompanies the gifts of God's grace.

Francis W. Parker says, "Art is the fundamental means of telling the truth."

De Rougemont says the purpose of art is to signify. He tells us that art has as its purpose "the bribing of attention, the magnetizing of the sensibility, the fascination of the meditation ... and at the same time, it must orient existence towards something which transcends sounds and forms, or ... words. ... It is a calculated trap for meditation and a trap made in order to catch something."

It is past time for the artists, writers, composers, novelists, artisans, architects and other artists of this generation of the children of the Kingdom to come forth.

In Gaebelein's book The Christian, The Arts, and Truth, he writes concerning God's great anointed artists and craftsmen:

> Do you know what the name Bezalel means? It means "in the shadow [or protection] of God." So here was a man who may well stand as the prototype, the example, of the Godly artist and craftsman in any field—a man, in this instance, to whom the Lord gave ability for a lofty purpose—to make known His truth through the construction of the Tabernacle. And, as his name implies, Bezalel lived and worked under the Lord's own shadow or patronage. Think of it! The Lord Himself the Divine Patron of the arts! How dare we, his creatures, ever look down on and neglect what He honored?

In Matthew 25. Jesus said every man is given talent, or ability. This talent is to be cultivated and used to glorify God and to enrich humanity. In the visual arts, you may be surprised by the myriad ways to accomplish this. Some of them are listed here for you: painting, drawing, print-making, photography, tapestry, embroidery, collage, montage, cartooning, writing, sculpture (stone, ceramic, metal, glass, ivory and bone, wood, wax, gems, paper, plastics and synthetics, and so on), goldsmithing, silversmithing, coppersmithing, bronze-casting, the clothing arts (the design and manufacture of garments and accessories for personal wear), tailoring, dressmaking, hat-making, glove-making, tool-making, furniture-making, book manufacture, toy-making, food preparation, interior design and decoration, display-making (decorative, educational displays to be used in libraries, museums, schools, churches and other locations of learning), commercial displays (to be used for advertising, merchandising and so on), architecture (temples, churches, monasteries, altars, pulpits, houses, palaces, apartments, monuments, theaters, hotels, libraries, schools, office buildings, shopping malls, stores and other structures), civil engineering (bridges, dams, highways, piers, harbors, aqueducts, viaducts, lighthouses, airplane fields and hangars, amusement parks, exhibitions and so on), seascaping and landscaping. Landscaping could include water design (fountains, pools and so on in relation to architecture and gardens), gardening, horticulture, flower arranging, and topiary art (the art of ornamental clipping and training of plants). And we're not done yet! You also could showcase your God-given artistic ability as a community designer, or a town, city, regional or urban planner. You could design parks, waterfronts or do environmental planning for your city. You might design bicycles, motorcycles, automobiles, trains, trailers, submarines, sailboats, airplanes, gliders, jets, rockets or hot air balloons.

Jesus Christ was also an artist. The Bible refers to Him as a carpenter (Mark 6:3). The Greek word for "carpenter" is tekton. It means artificer, craftsman, producer, to produce, bring forth. It is more accurately translated architect. Jesus is not merely a carpenter, He is an architect. Architecture is art. Jesus, the Savior of the world (John 4:42) is an artist and an architect. He used images of houses and mansions in His teaching (John 14:2). Is this unimportant? I don't think so.

Architecture has been defined as the concept or idea that uses the medium of building, the process or technique of building, to communicate. People have a choice of whether to visit a museum or to attend a concert. But everyone experiences architecture. Any new building in your town, city or neighborhood commands your attention. And since architecture communicates and teaches, we must raise up Kingdom architects. Architects design buildings from the perspective of their worldviews (Genesis 11:4-6). It has been written that architecture, as art that communicates, may in its communication be disturbing, inspiring, alienating or transcending, depending on the conscious or unconscious worldview and goals of those who design the structure. The soul and spirit of our cities have much to do with their architecture.

Architecture also has been called "living history." Architecture is influenced basically by seven things: worldview, needs, society, materials, technology, culture and climate. Architecture is one of the areas in which the Church has had practically nothing to say. An oblique commentary here and there on cramped urban dwelling conditions or on the limited availability of affordable housing is the word we have. We should lift our voices in these areas. However, we should do so understanding that this is reactionary. We must raise up prophetic architects who understand the spirit of building. Scripture teaches us that some architecture offends God, and He will lift His blessing from those involved in its design. God gave Moses, Bezalel, Aholiab and David revelation from the Holy Spirit as to how they were to design architecture that would please Him and that He would bless by bestowing His Glory upon the place.

God promised His covenant nation Israel beautiful houses full of good things (Deuteronomy 6:11, 8:12; Proverbs 3:33, 15:6, 19:14, 24:3). "Good" is the Hebrew word towb or tuwb. It means beautiful, bountiful, best, cheerful, pleasant, gracious, joyful, kindly, wealth, prosperity. There will be no ghettos in heaven. There will be no projects, no dilapidated dwellings that bruise the spirit of man and assault his God-given dignity. It is not a sin to own an architecturally resplendent, beautifully furnished, artistically landscaped home, with flowers, shrubs, pools and fountains. The image of God in us craves beauty. There is an anointing from the Holy Spirit to design architecture and build houses and other buildings that glorify our Father, the Maker and Master of the universe.

I am calling forth those of you called by the Spirit of God to minister to the spirit of man by designing beautiful buildings, houses, gardens, parks and waterfalls, not just for yourself, but for your city, your nation and your world. Let God use you to replace the ugly, the tawdry with beauty revealed and anointed by the Holy Spirit. There is an anointing from God to "bribe the attention, magnetize the sensibility, and fascinate the meditation." Kingdom artists have a divine call to be in the world but not of it. They have a prophetic call to the domain of color, sound, words, images, wind, water, fire, earth and so on. These things have been used to enslave the spirit and soul of men. Images have been used to limit the actualizing of human potential. The artist moves into the domain of sound and image and begins to bring those images and sounds captive to the obedience of Christ.

There are so many other modes of artistic expression through which you may give glory to God and release to the torrents of creative/artistic potential locked inside you. There is dance. There are numerous references to dancing in the Bible. Dance is central to many cultures. Dance is kinetic poetry. The body becomes the vehicle not just for spontaneous expressions of joy, but for the telling of stories, personal and collective. Alvin Ailey's Revelations never fails to move me, no matter how many times I see it. Dancing helped African slaves to stay alive. It helped to keep their spirits buoyant. Black dance, like black music, helped to shape the foundations of American culture. From William Henry "Juba" Lane to Elida Webb, the inventor of the Charleston, to Bill "Bojangles" Robinson to the Creative Dance Group of Hampton Institute to Alvin Ailey, Judith Jamison, the Hines, Savion Glover and many Pentecostal church services, dance is part of the cultural and religious expression of African-Americans and many other cultures.

The great actor Ira Aldridge was the first African-American to play Shakespeare's Macbeth, Shylock and King Lear. Aldridge became known as "the African Roscius," after the famous slave actor in ancient Rome, Quintus Roscius Gallus. He became somewhat of an icon in Russia, Prussia,

Germany, Austria and Serbia. King Frederick William IV of Prussia awarded Aldridge the Golden Medal for Art and Sciences. Only three individuals before Aldridge had been bestowed this honor. Then there was internationally renowned Paul Robeson. Robeson, actor, singer, scholar, linguist, Phi-Beta Kappa key holder, lawyer, historian, athlete and political activist, also played Shakespeare's Othello. Robeson used his enormous fame and gifts to address human rights violations worldwide.

Like these artists, an entire generation needs to know and understand the artistic call of God. There is a cry from the human spirit to be released into deep dimensions of the creative power of the Almighty. We speak forth and decree the release of the deep rivers of creative purpose and potential resident in the spirit of man (Proverbs 20:5). I am ecstatic and grateful to Father for allowing me to be alive in time of the release of prophetic destiny. It is a time literally of a creative explosion on behalf of the children of the Kingdom of God. Brilliant works of art, literature, music, cinema, architecture and numerous other art forms are about to be unleashed that display the majesty, the opulence, the unsurpassable greatness of our God and Father, of our Lord Jesus Christ and of the wonderful Holy Spirit.

10

THE FIRE OF SPORT

According to Fortune magazine, sports in America is a $156 billion-per-year industry. During a business trip once, I had a stopover in Orlando, Florida. I used the time between flights to browse a bookstore. The cover story for Fortune magazine (June 22, 1998) was titled "The Jordan Effect." The story's authors sought to calculate the impact of "the greatest basketball player who ever lived," and midas-touched pitchman Michael Jordan's impact on the U.S. economy. They concluded that Jordan's impact as an endorser was at $10 billion and counting. This is phenomenal. After all, Michael Jordan is not the president of the United States or the head of any other political kingdom. What he does as a basketball player is probably not going to affect the balance of power between nations or solve any of the world's seemingly intractable problems. No, Michael Jordan won't sign any major treaty that begins or ends a world war. But Jordan in a galaxy of less luminescent stars in the realm of sport touches us at an entirely different level. I make no pretense at being a sports psychologist or a sociologist of sport. I am, pure and simple, a fan—a fan with some opinions and observations about sport, but still a fan.

I respect Michael Jordan's work ethic, his will to win, to never make excuses. These are some of the same attributes I respect(ed) in Larry Bird, Ken Griffey, Jr., Cal Ripken, Jerry Rice and Troy Aikman, just to name a few of the many athletes I admire and respect.

I don't know how many sports fans watch sports on television and attend sports contests purely for entertainment. While viewing sports contests can be very entertaining, I am always looking to learn something. Some athletes, when it is all on the line, seem to be able to reach way down inside themselves and draw from the fire. They never make excuses, they play with pain, and they are perennial students of the technical and psychological contours of their sport. I watch Cynthia Cooper, Cheryl Swoopes, Lisa Leslie, Martina Hingis, Monica Seles and Venus Williams, Serena Williams or Tiger Woods and I see a psychological intensity and commitment to excellence that I want to emulate in all my endeavors.

For years, athletes in the former Soviet Union dominated because the former Soviets had pioneered in the study of the psychology of sport. Other nations and countries were training their athletes in physical strength and preparation, but not in mental strength and preparation. The Biblical proverb that says, As a man thinketh in his heart, so is he, applies as much to sport as to any other endeavor. Sport certainly involves training of the physical body and the development of physical strength. However, those who rise to the level of champions learn how to access another level. They learn how to identify and master the emotional and motivational aspects of sport. It has been said that sixty percent to ninety percent of success in sports in due to emotional and motivational factors. When superb physical training meets progressive mastery of the emotional and motivational forces of sport, one is prepared for uncanny performances.

Mihaly Csikszentmihalyi (pronounced Chick-sent-me-high) in his book Flow: The Psychology of Optimal Experience, writes, "The best moments usually occur when a person's body or mind is stretched to its limits in a voluntary effort to accomplish something difficult and worthwhile."

Many Christian thinkers and preachers of Christ's Gospel believe sport to be of complete inconsequence. I will grant that relative to eternity, sport is a less majesterial theme. But in the contemporary world in which we live, sport is an important part of culture. Whether one is a professional or semi-professional athlete, a regular weekend warrior or merely a spectator, sport touches most of us at some level. Furthermore, sport provides us with many analogies to everyday life.

Say you are a businessperson negotiating the largest deal in your company's history. Your staff has done all the preparation for game day. The competition has been scouted. Your game plan has been satisfactorily reviewed. Now it is on you! The final presentation is yours. The game is tied in the fourth quarter with thirty seconds on the game clock and twenty seconds on the shot clock. The play is designed for you. Do you want the ball? Will you take the shot? Do you believe you'll make the shot?

Most of us work with teams of one sort or another. We learn from sport how important it is to have confidence in the ability of your teammates. National Basketball Association executive, author and popular motivational speaker Pat Riley says, "Teamwork is the essence of life. ... Great teamwork is the only way to reach our ultimate moments, to create the breakthroughs that define our careers, to fulfill our lives with a sense of lasting significance." (Pat Riley, The Winner Within, Putnam, 1993)

Whether in sports, business, the arts or any other profession, a person is blessed if in life he or she has the opportunity to be part of a great achieving team. Even Jesus Christ, before he began His earthly ministry, selected His team. Pat Riley says, "Every team is a stage setting, a place to act out the drama of our lives. When our teams excel, we win. Our best efforts, combined with those of our teammates, grow into something far greater and far more satisfying than anything we could have achieved on our own."

For those Christian preachers and teachers who believe sport to be of no consequence, I point out the verse 2 Samuel 2:14, which says:

> And Abner said to Joab, "Let the young men now arise, and play before us." And Joab said, "Let them arise."

"Play" is the Hebrew word sachaq meaning to play or be in sports, pleasure. This refers to finding pleasure in sports. Of course, sports in the culture of Samuel's day was not a multi-billion-dollar-a-year industry with high-paid, high-profile athletes, celebrity product endorsements and the attendant culture of sport. Nevertheless, sport and pleasure derived from there, is mentioned in Scripture.

The Apostle Paul makes many references to sports in his epistles, particularly in 1 Corinthians 9:24-27. He mentions the games of Ephesus (2 Timothy 4:7), the contests of Olympia, which included boxing (Ephesians 4:27), chariot races and foot races (Romans 9:16, Galatians 2:2, Acts 20:24), and wrestling for men and children (Ephesians 6:12). By the time of the Greeks and Romans, victorious athletes would achieve celebrity status. Some of the most famous athletes of biblical times were charioteers. A champion charioteer had to possess tremendous strength, agility and a steely calmness of nerves. The training period of the charioteer was long and arduous.

The chariot was pulled by two horses that the charioteer took turns straddling during a race. As he waved weapons in mock warfare, the charioteer leaped from horse to horse. The greatest charioteers became very wealthy. It was not unusual for him to have his picture displayed throughout the city and to be treated as an idol. The frequency of athletic symbolism in Paul's writings probably indicates at least a mild enthusiasm for sports.

If you love to see the human being meld spirit, mind and body and soar to the outer reaches of achievement as I do, sports is certainly one of the realms in which this can happen. Because I am a teacher at heart, the study of what molds certain people into champion competitors while others remain couch potatoes fascinates me. In addition to being a teacher, I am also a coach. A coach creates a vision of greatness for the team. Coaches are a blend of optimism and realism. They set goals and implement ways by which progress toward the goals can be measured. They are students of human potential and motivation. They respect the players and the game. They master their domain and do not lead through intimidation. The coach helps the athlete/player to move closer toward his or her goal of being a champion and of playing on a great team.

This is why coaches fascinate me, whether it is Vince Lombardi, Tom Landry, Eddie Robinson, Rick Pitino, Pat Riley, Tony Dungee, John Wooden or Phil Jackson. The science, the art of coaching, of causing individuals to sacrifice, to push themselves to the limits physically and mentally to distinguish themselves as champions, is intriguing to me. The coach must balance an encyclopedic knowledge of the game and its intricacies with an understanding of human and group psychology. The game must be understood from the center outward. The coach must be a game strategist and must inspire superstars to sacrifice individual achievement for team accomplishment. The esteemed John Wooden taught that, "The main ingredient in stardom is the rest of the team."

He taught, "Talent is God-given; be humble. Fame is man-given; be thankful. Conceit is self-given; be careful."

As I have studied great athletes and great teams in sports history, a constant theme emerges as being crucial to success: mastery of the fundamentals. Webster's New World Dictionary defines fundamental as of or forming a foundation or basis, most important or chief, on which others are based, most important, a principle, theory, law, the root. Michael Jordan attributes the virtuosity of his game today to an early mastery of basketball fundamentals. Any truly virtuoso performance began with attention to the fundamentals. In golf, it begins with hitting thousands and thousands of balls all alone with no gallery to perfect one's swing. In baseball, it begins with the batter taking batting practice with only his hitting coach present. In football, it begins with the wide-receiver relentlessly pursuing the precision of his routes. Somewhere along the route, Troy Aikman mastered the art of staying in the pocket until the absolute last second until his receiver is open.

In basketball, there are shooting, ball-handling, defensive and rebounding fundamentals. Coach John Wooden said, "Basketball is a mental game, and this fact is probably more apparent in shooting than it is in any fundamental." How do great players handle shooting slumps? A player must possess more than great mechanics. You may aspire to greatness in sport. If so, realize there is a reason for every missed shot. Great coaches and students of the game tell us that shooting slumps often are related to the development of bad habits. Negative factors interfere with the normal sharpshooter's original shooting form. Physical or mental factors may be contributing to the slump. Maybe teams are playing really tough defense against you and not allowing you to get into your shooting rhythm. The thing to know is that the slump does not have to last. It will be largely up to you. To break the slump, you must never lose your confidence in yourself as a shooter. Study your mechanics and regain your original shooting form. Adjust your visualization technique. See the ball going into the basket. Mentally rehearse your perfect shooting rhythm and form. Spend time shooting the ball in practice to regain your form.

Slumps may happen in a variety of sports. The golfer misses the green or seems to be in a putting slump. The quarterback is overthrowing his receivers. The big-time home run hitter is struggling at the plate.

What about people who are in a slump in life? They are in a motivational slump and can't seem to get their lives off the ground. The same kinds of observation and adjustment strategies that worked for our shooting guard are applicable to life in general. You need to ponder, What kinds of negative influences have I allowed into my thinking? Am I governing my life in accordance with the principles in God's Word? Have I mastered the fundamentals? What are the fundamentals you need to master? In sports, in business, in life, it all begins with the Word of God.

The athlete must constantly monitor his or her intensity levels. Csikszentmihalyi says, "Optimal experience depends on the ability to control what happens in consciousness moment by moment." He says if we can control the information in our minds that represents all our experiences—joy, pain, interest, boredom and so on—we can control what our lives will be like. This obviously has application beyond sports. Csikszentmihalyi says the periods when we are struggling to overcome challenges are the periods we find to be the most enjoyable in life. He says, "By stretching skills, by reaching toward higher challenges, ... a person becomes an increasingly extraordinary person."

This is God's will for you. You were created to be extraordinary! Extraordinary means not according to the usual custom or regular plan; going beyond the ordinary degree, measure or limit; sent on a special errand. You are sent on a special errand by God. There is an area in which it is your destiny to perform superlatively.

The fire of sport involves understanding goal setting, expectations, dedication, responsibility, cultivating winning attitudes, developing Godly confidence, learning, preparing, visualizing, concentrating, developing mental toughness and understanding the way of the winner. To compete at our highest levels, we must master our emotions. Our performance reflects our emotions. Your emotional state affects the way you perceive the world around you and the very activity of your physical body. Everything from the way you speak to your heart rate is affected by emotions. The apostle Paul and the prophet Isaiah give us the Master's strategy for controlling emotions in Philippians 4:8 and Isaiah 26:3. Respectively, they say:

> Finally, brethren, whatsoever things are true, whatsoever things are honest, whatsoever things are just, whatsoever things are pure, whatsoever things are lovely, whatsoever things are of good report; if there be any virtue, and if there be any praise, think on these things (KJV).

> Thou wilt keep him in perfect peace, whose mind is stayed on thee: because he trusteth in thee (KJV).

Besides mastering his or her emotions, a great athlete seeks help from great teachers.

Ray B. Essick, executive director of United States Swimming, said, "It takes a great coach, parent, or friend to help an athlete take responsibility for striving to explore the limits of his or her talent. This responsibility encompasses training for peak fitness, developing excellent technique, and most importantly, learning to compete." Some of these lessons are difficult to teach in a society where mediocrity, unprofessionalism and shoddiness have become so prevalent. From retail to manufacturing, from food service to transportation, mediocrity threatens industry and profit. Sport remains a venue in which principles of discipline, respect for authority, hard work, teamwork, commitment to excellence, sacrifice, punctuality and overcoming adversity can be taught.

In his book Adversity Quotient, Paul G. Stoltz writes, "We are born with a core human drive to ascend. ... I use the term ascend in the broadest sense—moving your purpose in your life forward no matter what your goals." Stoltz says that one's capacity to succeed in life is proportional to one's ability to handle adversity. Among other things, Stoltz says our ability to handle adversity affects our performance, motivation, productivity, learning, energy, attitude and persistence. As stated earlier in this chapter, sport involves all these mental and emotional states. Sport involves learning to handle adversity. A loss in the big game. The season-ending injury. The bad call by an official. A hostile sports writer. The cheap shot hit. The irate, verbally abusive fan. Teammates who don't share your hunger for or dedication to winning. The demotion from your starting position. The adversity you handle not only in sports but in life is helping to prepare you for the further unfolding of your destiny. You are a tough competitor who possesses a high Adversity Quotient (ability to bounce back from adversity). You are not a quitter. You are a winner.

Sport is one domain where you often see large grown men cry. When they have pushed themselves to the top mental and physical brink of their existence, their careers are winding down, and they have yet to win a championship. And you know what? Grown men all over America cry with them. Maybe it is because the media brings these athletes into our homes for games, personal interviews and so on, and we often feel we know them. We identify with the frustration, with trying to put losing into perspective. We identify with watching the opposition enjoy the fruits of victory while we try to muster the courage to persuade mind and body to do it all again. Yet while we never completely embrace losing, we learn to accept it when we've given our best. We know when we have left blood, sweat, tears and championship effort on the field, court, diamond, track or links.

In life, church, sport and business, how do we cultivate an atmosphere of winning? The coach is central to this process. He or she creates an environment where people want to win. The winning environment provides challenges, along with the tools to meet the challenges. Fulfillment and joy are felt when the challenges are met. Challenges met and victories realized are celebrated. The winning atmosphere is one where a set of values is shared by everyone in the organization from the owners to the coaching staff, athletes, trainers, administration, and public relations and front office staff.

One of the most difficult yet important decisions involving creating and maintaining the winning atmosphere is knowing when a certain individual athlete, coach or other individual does not fit with the team's chemistry. The decision to release that person must be made without delay and done in such a manner as to respect the person's dignity, professional integrity and professional future. For the team or organization to be successful, its vision, values, mission and goals must be understood, embraced and supported by all.

Over the years, The University of Notre Dame has cultivated an atmosphere of academic excellence and winning at football. With such great coaches as Knute Rockne, Frank Leahy, Ara Parseghian and Lou Holtz, the Notre Dame football program has become the stuff of which legends are made. Each of these coaches brought a unique genius to Notre Dame football. Rockne was passionately committed to teaching fundamentals, though he was one of football's great innovators. He was a master motivator relentlessly driven by a strong sense of vision, great enthusiasm and admirable sportsmanship. Leahy, intense and driven, lived football twenty-four hours a day, seven days a week. He was intolerant of players who did not want to reach their potential. He deeply cared about his players and took keen interest in their lives beyond football. Parseghian, olympic in preparation, was intensely focused and extremely competitive. Then there's Holtz, known as a man of integrity who harbors a sheer passion for the competition of football, a thoughtful man and one who can work you under the table. These men are all part of a legacy of excellence and winning.

Rockne was once asked to name the greatest team he'd ever had. He replied, "I'll find out what my best team is when I find out how many doctors and lawyers and good husbands and good citizens have come off each and every one of my teams." This puts the role of sport and of coaching into perspective. Part of the glory of sport is its ability to transcend itself. It's about the competition, but it's also about life and the lessons you learn in the trenches. It's about applying the lesson one learns to the task of becoming a better person.

Joe Paterno, the great Penn State head football coach, said, "Many people, particularly in sports, think of success and excellence as though they are the same. They are not. Success is perishable and often outside our control. In contrast, excellence is something that's lasting, dependable, and largely within a person's control." Paterno, who has won two national titles at Penn State, often challenges his team by telling them, "If you want to be a national championship football team, every single day of your life you've got to do something that challenges your body and teaches you more about the game. Every single day. If you're not ready to commit yourself to excellence, there are too many really fine football squads in this country that will prevent you from becoming number one."

Former San Francisco Forty-Niners and Hall of Fame football coach Bill Walsh won three Super Bowls. He is known as a football genius. Walsh says to overcome adversity, one needs an inner confidence that has been tested. He says this self-confidence has to have been molded by defeat, has to have been shaken, absorbed punishment and developed a toughness that will take on anything, survive and win. Walsh says the coach's most important function is that of teacher. He says standards of performance and behavior must be set to ensure success. Walsh says a head coach must believe his or her abilities can and will make a difference. This is an important principle. Many leaders today are laboring with all their might in sincerity, but they do not believe their abilities and efforts are making a difference. It is a painful sight to see leaders who no longer believe that abilities or efforts are achieving anything. Walsh subscribes to Coach John Wooden's maxim that, "Without organization and leadership towards a realistic goal, there is no chance of realizing more than a small percentage of your potential." Walsh was a meticulous organizer who scripted entire games and thought through what the team would do in particular game scenarios. He planned for a "wide range of small and large disasters ... reducing the potential for you and others to be caught off guard—you can actually be more aggressive, and thus more likely to avert setbacks. Having planned for the worst, you can do a lot more than hope for the best."

Before you write this off as being negative thinking, you should ponder its wisdom as it relates to sport and to life in general. To conceive certain game scenarios and what the team might do in each of them is a wise strategy. If the players practice these scenarios, if they present themselves in a game situation, the players and coaches will be confident in what to do. This could mean a last-minute victory. Concentration and focus, Walsh taught, are two key factors in overcoming the barriers to success.

Often in life at the first sign of a setback, many of us are prepared to abandon our game plans. It's been said that, "Every adversity carries with it the seed of an equivalent or greater benefit." Once you have skillfully developed your game plan or life plan, don't be so quick to throw it away. Great teams and great athletes don't achieve success by being easily intimidated and turning away from their game plans. Flexibility is required, of course, but don't be moved by fear.

Study your opponents' strengths and weaknesses. Assess not only their talent level, but the level of their mental preparation and their will to win as a team. Master the fundamentals, and make sure you are always mentally prepared to compete. All successful teams need:

A clear, concise mission statement.

A corporate philosophy.

Simple, clear, measurable goals.

Accountability.

A commitment to excellence.

Strong, visionary leadership.

Audrus Barzdukas says, "Sport is the personification of human drama and learning. ... We want to understand ... why one team or individual was better than another. We want to determine what strategy had the greatest influence on the competition's outcome." Why do certain teams or individuals put together consistent championship runs over periods of time? The answer is not simply talent. At a certain level, all athletes possess talent. Barzdukas offers an explanation: "You control your destiny. It is that simple. Better than anyone else, you know what you want and how you are going to get it. You can be great, mediocre or awful at whatever you choose to do because you govern your mindset. A solid commitment to become incrementally better in some area may take your team to the next level. It seems as though part of the difference between champions and others lies in the recesses of the mind."

Hunger is part of the mindset of champions. In the period between Olympic competitions, swimmers swim more than 7,000 miles and spend more than 750 hours lifting weights. Three key components in developing the champion mindset are desire, preparation and action. Great athletes and teams have a fire in them burning to excel. The desire to excel is channeled into preparation, then that preparation allows them to perform at optimal levels. Champions in any area of sport—and life—are confident people. The Bible also has something to say about confidence:

> Cast not away therefore your confidence, which hath great recompence of reward. For ye have need of patience, that, after ye have done the will of God, ye might receive the promise (Hebrews 10:35, 36, KJV).

The Greek word for confidence is parrhesia (par-rhay-see-ah). It means assurance, boldness, to pour forth, speak, command, say in assurance. Another Greek word for confidence is hupostasis, meaning support, essence, substance. The Hebrew word mibtach (mib-tawkh) is translated confidence and means security, certainty, assurance, hope.

When you are performing in the zone of an area where God has gifted you, you should be confident and secure. Preparation always helps to bolster confidence. To succeed in sport, you must be confident. When you know that you have given everything to preparation, your mental focus is superb and your mind won't betray you with haunting thoughts of skipped practice sessions. Confident athletes trust both their ability and preparation. Confident athletes have what Coach Walsh called tried inner confidence. They have handled the pressure, so they know they can handle it.

I like what Barzdukas wrote in the book GoldMinds:

Greatness begins with understanding the power of freedom, for freedom empowers you with the ability to choose what you want to do and how well you want to do it.

It is not your coaches, teammates, friends, business associates or competitors who ultimately determine how well you will be at what you do. That decision is yours. Jesus said, "According to your faith be it unto you" (Matthew 9:29, KJV). You choose how good you will be by setting your own level of desire, preparation and action. You will set your own level of commitment. The process of training to be a champion will take years, maybe decades, but you will remain relentlessly focused. You will invest time in visualizing your greatness. During visualization—a powerful technique—remember these important points:

Relax.

Use all your senses (hear the sounds, smell the grass, the court or other environment, hear the cheers, the announcer, the starters pistol).

- Be vivid. (Use technicolor imagery.)

- Focus on proper technique.

- Visualize daily.

- Use great detail in your visualization.

- See yourself always giving your best performance.

Stay positive, and have faith and confidence.

Remember, preparation ensures confidence.

When wife, mother and attorney Sue Cobb decided she would climb Mount Everest, many people thought she had gone crazy. She tells her story in her book The Edge of Everest: A Woman Challenges the Mountain. At 29,028 feet, Mount Everest is the highest mountain in the world. Many have died attempting to scale its summit. But Cobb was determined. In the minds of many, Mount Everest represents the "death of the impossible." In other words, when you have climbed Everest, there remain no impossibilities for you. Philip J. Davis and David Park have said, "The door to the invisible must be visible." The next level of performance and confidence for us all lies behind something we can see. In the case of Sue Cobb, it was the mighty mountain.

On the matter of preparation and confidence, she tells a story in her book of being in a valley looking up at peaks on either side in the twenty-two thousand- to twenty-four thousand-foot range. She aptly called this valley the Valley of Despair. Conditions were slippery, terrain was irregular and jagged, with stratified rock, and she was physically and mentally exhausted. Despite it all, she wrote something powerful about her climbing companions: "Courtney and Bob have years of living and teaching survival in arctic conditions, and they know my capabilities, so I have confidence in their judgment. I'm also convinced that if it is at all possible, they will give me a chance to go to the top." They made it! Why? In part because they were confident. Why? Because they were prepared.

In 1990, Bill Irwin hiked 2,168.9 miles through four-teen states on the famed Appalachian Trail. You might say, "Okay, so what's the big deal?" Well, the big deal is Irwin is blind. His faithful guide dog Orient accompanied him as he became the first blind person to hike the entire Appalachian Trail. To me, this is perhaps more incredible than winning the Super Bowl, the NBA championship, the Stanley Cup, the Heavyweight Championship of the World or the Masters. What a feat of indomitable courage, faith, strength and deter-mination. Irwin, in his book Blind Courage, wrote: "I never had any doubts that God had called me to hike the Appalachian Trail. As strange as it must have sounded to oth-ers, my sense of being on a divine mission was solidly con-firmed before Orient and I left."

Sue Cobb and Bill Irwin are champion athletes. So is Sir Ranulph Fiennes. Fiennes and his partner crossed Antarctica—one thousand, three hundred fifty miles pulling five hundred-pound sleds in temperatures of minus eighty-six degrees Fahrenheit. In spite of treacherous frostbite, starva-tion, and mental and emotional torment, they persisted to achieve their goal. In his book Mind Over Matter, Fiennes writes:

As far as determination is concerned, any human being, however meek and unambitious they may think themselves, can develop and nurture a single-minded desire to fulfill a particular goal. The quantum leap is the moment of instiga-tion, that first push to make the stone roll.

You do not need to climb Mount Everest, hike the Appalachian Trail or cross Antarctica to be a champion. But there is some level of competitive excellence in you waiting to be tapped. There is another level of sheer grit, another whole dimension of performance at your particular sport. What price are you willing to pay to be a champion?

What can you do to elevate the play of your teammates? How can you develop and maintain an attitude of excellence and the indomitable will to win. You can lead by example by practicing with the same intensity you bring to the game. You can become a student of your sport. Has your position ever been played to the outer limits? It has been said that a genius is a person who looks at what others are looking at and sees something different. Let that genius be you.

Sport has its poetic or jazz-like moments. Michael Jordan's moves to the basket could be called riffs instead of moves. It's jazz, beebop, funk and rap. It's ballet, tap and creative dance. It's prose and poetry. It's competition and compassion, fire and ice, joy and sorrow, laughter and tears. It's greatness of the heart, exhaustion and celebration. It's sport, and it is The Fire Inside!

Author Contact:

James L. Giles

James Giles International

P.O. Box 480339

Charlotte, North Carolina 28269

Office (704) 948-0039

Fax (704) 948-8005

E-mail: jamesgiles04@aol.com